The Rehabilitation of Sexual Offenders

Sexual offenders – arguably the most hated and feared of all offenders – commit their crimes in our communities and are then hidden from public view as they serve long prison sentences. However, despite the public's understandable anxiety, our criminal justice systems hold to the premise that almost all offenders have the right to hope for rehabilitation, even redemption. Therefore the majority of sexual offenders return to live in our communities, closely monitored by criminal justice agencies and subject to rigorous controls.

This book provides an authoritative guide to working with sexual offenders, with a focus on managing those who are reintegrating into the community. It includes those with the most striking histories of trauma and psychological difficulty, and those who have previously failed in their attempts at resettlement. It covers helpful theoretical ideas, such as attachment theory and models of desistance, as well as the latest evidence base for good quality risk assessment.

The book supports practitioners on the front line of this work by providing them with evidence-based guidance. It presents a multitude of case examples and practice tips that can support effective decision making and achieve safe outcomes, as well as help such offenders build worthwhile community lives.

Dr. Jackie Craissati MBE is a Consultant Clinical and Forensic Psychologist and has worked as a leader in the field of offending, risk and mental disorder for over 25 years.

The Rehabilitation of Sexual Offenders

Complexity, Risk and Desistance

Jackie Craissati

Routledge
Taylor & Francis Group

LONDON AND NEW YORK

First published 2019
by Routledge
2 Park Square, Milton Park, Abingdon, Oxon OX14 4RN

and by Routledge
711 Third Avenue, New York, NY 10017

Routledge is an imprint of the Taylor & Francis Group, an informa business

© 2019 Jackie Craissati

British Library Cataloguing-in-Publication Data
A catalogue record for this book is available from the British Library

Library of Congress Cataloging-in-Publication Data
Names: Craissati, Jackie, author.
Title: The rehabilitation of sexual offenders : complexity, risk and
    desistance / Jackie Craissati.
Description: Abingdon, Oxon ; New York, NY : Routledge, 2019. |
    Includes bibliographical references and index.
Identifiers: LCCN 2018025158| ISBN 9781138570634 (hb : alk. paper) |
    ISBN 9781138570641 (pb : alk. paper) | ISBN 9780203703342 (eb)
Subjects: LCSH: Sex offenders—Rehabilitation—Great Britain.
Classification: LCC HV6593.G7 C73 2019 | DDC 365/.661—dc23
LC record available at https://lccn.loc.gov/2018025158

ISBN: 978-1-138-57063-4 (hbk)
ISBN: 978-1-138-57064-1 (pbk)
ISBN: 978-0-203-70334-2 (ebk)

Typeset in Bembo
by Swales & Willis Ltd, Exeter, Devon, UK

Contents

Figures

Tables

Acknowledgements

I would like to thank all the Challenge group facilitators who have formed the pulsing heart of the project over the past 25 years; it is as a result of your dedication that we have achieved the results we have (as well as only having cancelled three sessions in all that time!). So thanks go to Anand, Belinda, Caoimhe, Chris, Ethel, Felicity, Jake, Jenni, Jo, Joan, John, Karen, Kyati, Lisa, Maggie, Marianna, Mark, Matt, Ophelia, Patricia, Philip, Pretty, Rebecca, Richard, Ruth, Stuart, Theresa.

My thanks also go to all the men with sexual offences who have engaged with me whilst embarking on the bumpy path to an offence-free life; our collaborative relationship has not always been straightforward; at times it has been challenging, occasionally completely exasperating. But ultimately, I acknowledge the courage it has taken to allow me access to your most shameful actions and private fears, and the resolute determination that desisting from offending demands.

Finally I would like to express my gratitude to Heather Wood for her help in ensuring that Chapter 4 is acceptably true to the psychoanalytic model, and to Jessica Yakeley for her comments on an earlier draft of the book.

1 Setting the scene

Promoting the role of clinically applied research, and integrating this with learning from 'failure'

Sexual offenders – arguably the most abhorred of all offenders – commit their crimes in our communities and are then hidden from public view as they serve long custodial sentences. However, despite the public's aversion – powerfully expressed via the media throughout Europe and North America – our criminal justice systems hold to the premise that almost all offenders have the right to hope for rehabilitation, even redemption.

The majority of sexual offenders are therefore living in our communities, pursuing lives 'under the radar' in the hope of avoiding public exposure and retaliation, closely monitored by criminal justice agencies and subject to rigorous controls. Meanwhile, the public stubbornly adheres to myths regarding the monstrous and 'other' nature of sexual offenders, different to ourselves, dangerous and predatory. These myths are perpetuated by the current focus on high profile revelations, and recent scandals that have rocked both the UK and the USA (Figure 1.1 outlines some headlines captured on websites): for example, in the UK, the exposure of the celebrity Jimmy Savile[1] as an aggressively predatory and prolific child sexual abuser who manipulated the public and terrorised his victims, has understandably reinforced public abhorrence and intolerance of sexual offending behaviour; the exposure of prolific sexual abuse of children by Catholic priests horrified Americans; and most recently, on both sides of the Atlantic, the media has been filled with controversial disclosures of sexual misdemeanours in high profile public arenas.

The stakes are high, misconceptions abound, and the public is unforgiving. Those who are tasked with the duty of managing sexual offenders on behalf of the public – most notably the probation and police service, but also social workers and healthcare staff – bear the burden of an anxiety-provoking responsibility and fear exposure and public disapprobation if found to have failed in their duty of public protection.

Jimmy Savile: Scotland Yard labels Savile a 'prolific, predatory' sex offender after its investigation reveals 214 criminal offences across 28 police forces, between 1955 and 2009 (2013); Department of Health publishes the results of investigations by 28 medical establishments – in Leeds General Infirmary Savile abused 60 people including at least 33 patients aged from five to 75 (2014).

America's sexual-assault epidemic: the **Harvey Weinstein** scandal rocking Hollywood has now spread throughout the American Business world (2017)

British Parliament rocked by allegations of rape, sexual assault and drunken groping (2017).

John Geoghan, former priest, sexually abused approximately 130 boys; Church officials ordered him to get treatment or transferred him, but kept him on as a priest. Geoghan was found guilty of molesting a boy in 2002 and sentenced to prison; a year later he died after an attack by another inmate.

Figure 1.1 Extracts of media reports on high profile sexual abuse cases

The aim of this book is to provide an authoritative guide to working with sexual offenders, with a focus on managing those who are reintegrating into the community. Most particularly, the book aims to support those practitioners on the front line of this work by providing them with evidence based information and guidance that can support defensible decision making. The pragmatic and practical focus – with case vignettes and management advice – aims to build confidence and competence in achieving clarity and objectivity within a hostile public context.

As a practitioner, I have been based in the UK, working with offenders in the health and the criminal justice services. The book is therefore written from a UK perspective, but wherever appropriate and relevant, references to a North American perspective are been made.

The scope of the problem

Much has been written about the scope of the problem in terms of the sexual victimisation of children and women, and a wide range of data is available from sites such as the National Society for the Protection of Children (www.nspcc.org.uk) or the Office of Justice (ojp.gov) statistics. The aim here is simply to provide the current picture, as demonstrated by two key sets of figures: crime surveys and official conviction data. The Crime Survey for England and Wales is generally held to be the 'gold standard' of crime surveys and far more indicative of the true crime rate than official police and court records (see National Crime Victimization Survey for US figures (https://www.bjs.gov)). There are difficulties in directly comparing America to the UK, because of different survey methodologies; for example, the US Department of Justice largely collapses sexual and non-sexual violence into a single category, and does not provide detailed statistics related to sexual crimes. However, the latest survey in 2016 (Morgan & Kena, 2017) found that there were 1.2 sexual victimisations in the USA per 1,000 of the population, and that only 23% of these offences were reported to the police. The National Violence Against Women Survey in 2005 (Tjaden & Thoennes, 2006) estimated that only 10% of rapes were reported to the police at that point in time, of which 37% led to prosecution and 18% to a conviction for rape.

In England and Wales, the last detailed published report on sexual offences, drawn from the Crime Survey for 2016 (Office of National Statistics, 2017), analysed responses for 50,000 adults living in private households in England and Wales, and included sections on the nature of abuse as a child, and experience of sexual victimisation as adults. Key statistics include:

- 3% of women and < 1% of men reported being sexually assaulted in the past year, and this overall rate of 2% has been fairly consistent for the past ten years or so.
- 20% of women report having been sexually assaulted at some point since the age of 16, with the most common assaults taking the form of indecent exposure or unwanted touching, although 1/3 of the allegations related to penetrative assaults; of these, 40% were described as 'domestic-abuse-related;' that is perpetrated by someone within the family.
- 4% of men report having been sexually assaulted at some point since the age of 16 with 10% of these allegations related to penetrative assaults of which 5% were domestic-abuse-related.

When the adult survey sample were then asked about experiences of sexual victimisation in childhood:

- 11% of women and 3% of men reported being sexually assaulted in childhood (7% overall), the majority of assaults comprising indecent exposure and unwanted touching although 2% related to penetrative acts.
- interestingly 23% of those sexually abused by penetration as children went on to be sexually assaulted by penetration as adults, compared

to 3% of the total survey sample who became victims of sexually penetrative assaults as adults but who were not sexually abused as children. This pattern was far more marked for women (27%) as compared to men (3%), suggesting – from a psychological point of view – that adult men, previously victimised as children, may express their distress or otherwise act out trauma and disturbance in other ways, including becoming a perpetrator.

Although the crime survey strongly suggests that the rates of sexual crime have remained steady, the data on recorded crime – alleged offences reported to the police – tell another story (Office for National Statistics, 2018). The following data is formally described as crimes, but describes allegations, unless reference is made to convictions. In 2017:

- 138,045 sexual crimes were recorded by police, an increase of 23% from 2016 (figures for recorded sexual crimes have been going up since 2012)
- 27% of recorded sexual crime is for offences that have taken place more than a year previously, an increase of 28% from 2016
- rape, specifically, had gone up 22% in terms of the number of recorded crimes
- 37% of the allegations related to child sexual offences.

The data does not confirm that more crimes have been committed; it suggests that people are increasingly willing to come forward to report sexual crimes, and the ONS suggests that this may well be linked to publicity surrounding Operation Yewtree in 2012, the police investigation into sexual abuse allegations surrounding Jimmy Savile and other media personalities, scandals that I have already touched on. It may also reflect the improved approach by the police to recording crime following on from an inspection showing that an estimated one in four sexual offences that should have been recorded as crimes were not (HMIC, 2014). However, it still appears to be difficult to convert recorded sexual offences into convicted crimes. Official statistics for 2017 indicate that only 8% of recorded sexual crime leads to charges, and this rate rises to 15% when outcomes are added that were outstanding the previous year (Home Office, 2017). Unfortunately, although people are coming forward, more than 50% of the recorded crime suffers from evidential problems – including the victim not wishing to take matters forward – and this tendency is increasing in line with the rise in recorded sexual crime.

More encouraging, once a sexual allegation is proceeded with, there is around a 55% conviction rate (7,000 convictions in 2016/17), 60% of which lead to a custodial sentence averaging 60 months duration. If we consider the specific conviction of rape, for example, of the 5190 rape charges that were proceeded with in 2016/17, 2991 (58%) resulted in a sexual conviction, of which 1,532 (51%) were for rape, and the rest for lesser charges (Crown Prosecution Service, 2017). To provide some comparison with other offender types, there were around 30,000 proceedings for offences of violence against the person, with a 75% conviction rate, 40% of which led to a custodial sentence, averaging 22 months duration. Sexual offenders are clearly receiving increasingly long sentences and, although the figures fluctuate over time, they now comprise around 16% of the England and Wales prison population, at around 14,000 prisoners.

Despite the punitive response of the criminal justice system, it still remains the case that the majority of sexual offenders are residing in the community, either because they received a community sentence, or because they progressed through a long custodial sentence back into the community. In England and Wales, the number of prisoners with indeterminate sentences has also doubled over the past year, and yet we still only have around 60 individuals who have received a 'whole life' tariff for this sentence; the remaining 11,000 or will almost all be released eventually.

A note about complexity

This book focuses on complex sexual offenders and there are good reasons for taking this approach. As I hope **Chapter 2** on risk assessment will convincingly demonstrate, the majority of convicted sexual offenders do not go on to re-offend once convicted; they pose a low to moderate likelihood of further sexual re-offending. There are, of course, caveats to this statement as it can be very difficult for victims to come forward, and even more difficult to secure sufficient evidence to obtain a conviction. The section above demonstrates these difficulties. Nevertheless, although the assertion that the majority of convicted sexual offenders are moderately low risk and do not reoffend once convicted may appear to be provocative at first sight, there is growing evidence that our current community risk management approaches are managing risk effectively and sexual recidivism rates are falling (Thornton & d'Orazio, 2016). It is therefore reasonable to assert that the majority of sexual offenders released into the community can be managed with modest and common sense controls, such as restricting their access to particularly vulnerable potential victims.

Understanding why the majority of sexual offenders do not go on to re-offend requires a familiarity with both the risk literature (Chapter 2) and the theory concerning the underlying motives for sexual offending; this latter point is addressed later in this chapter, and in subsequent chapters. Therefore, the starting point for defining complexity is a focus on high risk sexual offenders; that is, those who pose a high likelihood of sexual recidivism relative to other sexual offenders.

I have chosen to highlight two further features of complexity in this book: the first is personality, often described somewhat controversially as personality disorder, but perhaps better understood as pervasive and persistent psychological difficulties. **Chapter 3** explores the issues of personality dysfunction, the ways in which it can develop out of childhood developmental experiences and adversity, and its relevance to risk and management in sexual offenders. The second area of concern is sexual deviance, sometimes referred to in the psychodynamic literature as 'perversion.' These are potentially derogatory terms but, when used carefully and precisely, describe a sub group of sexual offenders who habitually sexualise their aggressive impulses and emotional states, often expressed in terms of sexual preferences that we might all acknowledge as outside the current norms of accepted behaviour. Such preferences do not have to be illegal, and may not cause distress to others, but in the context in which we are discussing such 'deviance,' we are considering dominant sexual preferences – for example, for violent sexual encounters, or for pre-pubertal children – that are illegal and cause harm to others. **Chapter 4** examines the theoretical underpinning of sexual deviance or 'perversion' with particular reference to the psychoanalytical literature, a theoretical model that has fallen out of favour, but that has much to offer in understanding and managing complexity in sexual offenders.

Terminology

I have already intimated above that there are controversies relating to labels that are open to misinterpretation or have derogatory connotations. There are also multiple options for terminology in relation to sexual offenders; at different times they can be offenders, prisoners, patients, service users or clients; much depends on the context. For simplicity, I will refer to sexual offenders, and sometimes, where appropriate, to perpetrators (of the offence). When speaking specifically about those perpetrators with child victims, I will refer to child sexual abusers and I refer to those with adult victims as rapists. The latter descriptive term is not necessarily the same as the legal term with which they have been convicted (for example, rape is a charge that can relate to adult or child victims), but the term is less cumbersome than other options.

Although Chapter 2 focuses specifically on risk assessment, I return to this issue throughout the book. References to risk will always mean the likelihood of future offending behaviour, rather than the potential for harm or impact, unless specifically stated. Related to this, there is potential for confusion in the use of terminology for re-offending, re-arrest or reconviction. On balance, I have chosen to use the term recidivism, as it is internationally recognised as the term to describe the new crimes committed by a known criminal, and to use the term to denote new convictions (rather than new behaviours, whether caught or not). Any deviation from this fairly tight definition of recidivism will be highlighted.

I will always use the male pronoun, and the overwhelming focus of the book is on male sexual offenders. However, where there is pertinent literature on the small number of convicted female sexual offenders, then I will refer to them specifically.

Considering victims

This is not a book about victims and I do not apologise for this. In my experience, it is not particularly helpful to try and do justice to both perpetrators and victims within the same volume; I think this reflects the reality of trying to work with sexual offenders, and the struggle to contain our emotions – angry vengeful feelings – that ensue if as practitioners we have too close a contact with the distress of victims. It is the role of a psychologist – as scientist-practitioner – to bring an objective perspective to the issue of perpetrators; the task is not a moral or political one, and there are others – such as judges and politicians – who hold society's mandate in terms of punishment. I do, however, acknowledge that a central thrust of this book – engaging in a curious and empathic collaboration with sexual offenders in order to understand them – may be experienced by victims as collusive and dismissive of their traumatic experiences. Nevertheless, the position I take in this book is quite clear: our role in rehabilitating and managing sexual offenders in the community is first and foremost to ensure that there are no future victims; it is imperative that the focus is on minimising harm, but in order to achieve this, we need to engage with the world view of the sexual offender, and understand what motivates him; and to draw on the evidence base to be clear as to what it might be that enables him to desist from further harm. The victim is present in this work, but indirectly so, via victim statements and court documents, and it is important to re-visit this documentation regularly in order to ensure that we continue to hold the victim in mind.

Introducing the Challenge Project

The Challenge Project is the name of a community assessment and treatment programme for sexual offenders in London, UK, from which much of the clinical focus in this book is drawn. It has always been run as a partnership between the probation service and the forensic mental health service, and was initially conceptualised as an initiative local to south east London, with the aim of offering some group therapy to child sexual offenders in the vicinity. It has grown over the past 25 years to become the longest running community sex offender group in the UK, expanded to cover the whole of the Greater London area, and increasingly focused on the highest risk and most psychologically disordered sex offenders being released into the region. This happened in a rather organic manner, but was probably driven by four important ingredients:

- The project was supported in the early 1990s by a two-year research grant that forced us to think about a robust evaluative approach from its conception onwards; maintaining this valuable database has been relatively easy, and although our focus has changed over the years, we have never ceased to collect the relevant data.
- Having started the group programme, we never stopped for 24 years (indeed, we have only cancelled three sessions in that time), and we provided the attention that is required to ensure that referrals keep coming, the sexual offenders keep attending, the therapists are supported, and above all, we scrutinise and manage risk at all times. This is not about resources, as we have limited funds, but it is about stringent oversight and attention to detail.
- We have rigorously examined our own effectiveness, drawing on the database – painfully so at times – regularly reviewing the programme and the way in which we deliver it as a result of our findings.
- We take the view that we are only as good as our last failure, and we pay much more attention to our failures than our successes. Every participant recalled to prison or reconvicted is visited, followed up and where possible, welcomed back. We adjust our programme in light of these failures, each time striving to improve our outcomes.

Clinically applied research has been absolutely central to the success of our programme. This term refers to an integration of scientific theories with clinical experience in order to investigate and solve specific clinical/practice-related problems; in this instance, to find the most effective means of managing and/or treating complex sexual offenders in order to significantly reduce sexual recidivism. Large scale basic research studies are important in providing objective evidence and general trends against which smaller services can benchmark themselves; but they often lack the individualised detail that can assist the practitioner with decisions regarding individual sexual offenders. On the other hand, taking an individualised approach based on clinical experience alone can lead to serious errors of judgement, usually driven by the practitioner's belief in the validity of his/her approach; we all tend to make the grave mistake of assuming that the absence of failure in a particular case must mean that it was our intervention that was the key to success. The crucial importance of clinically applied research is that it challenges practitioner assumptions and creates opportunities for more effective approaches.

The benefits of clinically applied research in the Challenge Project became apparent after we completed the longer term follow up of the first 310 subjects in our programme (Craissati, South & Bierer, 2009); after coding the data independently, I was able to scrutinise the outcomes of the sexual offenders that I previously held under my care; I was astounded most of all to see who had not apparently sexually recidivated despite having caused grave concerns at the time of their assessment. A key moment was when we evaluated the impact of the group programme and found that it appeared to have no impact whatsoever on sexual recidivism; overcoming despondency and a strong inclination to argue away the findings, we explored the data further and we were able to demonstrate a significant impact of treatment on recidivism rates, but only in higher risk and more psychologically disordered sexual offenders. We shifted the criteria for our programme and the orientation of the therapy as a result, but as clinicians, it was not always easy to stand firm and exclude needy low risk sexual offenders from the group programme. This move towards a more risky group of sexual offenders in treatment posed significant challenges to our organisations, particularly the health service: that is, as we improved our capacity to have a significant and positive impact on reducing sexual recidivism rates in those who completed treatment, paradoxically the actual sexual recidivism rate increased (as the predicted base rate of recidivism increased)! Nevertheless, we stabilised our outcomes over the subsequent decade of treatment and, by altering the focus of treatment to better meet the needs of personality disordered offenders, we also improved the treatment completion rate. Our most recent shift has been to include those more antisocial and aggressive rapists, with the highest rates of prior failure. Very recent evaluation of this change has identified that we are losing significantly more group members before the end of treatment – they are recalled to prison for rule breaking and provocative behaviours – and although our sexual recidivism rate is stable, failures are occurring quicker and are exclusively related to high risk child sexual abusers who are accessing social media and illegal images. So our current thinking is urgently focused on tackling this problem.

Summing up the learning for us from clinically applied research on our sex offender programme, I would probably make the following observations:

- Evaluation can be painful, be prepared to face up to negative findings.
- There is no better learning or more humbling experience than following up your assessment conclusions to check much later as to whether you were right; we are dealing with people's lives (perpetrators and potential victims) and have an ethical duty to be as accurate as we can in our opinions.
- Making a difference means exposing your service to higher failure rates; it is all too easy to slip into accepting those sexual offenders into treatment who are motivated and compliant, and in doing so make false assumptions about effectiveness. Listen to the offender; if he is failing (re-offending, or recalled to prison) then there is something about the intervention that requires adjustment.

Table 1.1 Twenty-five years of sexual offender management

Dates	Key events	Challenge Project developments
1993–95	Treatment literature focuses on cognitive distortions, relapse prevention approaches (based on addiction models) and intimacy deficits	Group work programme is rolled out in south east London, with child sexual abusers only.
	Basic sex offender treatment group programmes (SOTP) are rolled out across prisons and community probation teams in England and Wales	Receipt of research funding for two years means that a comparison between the group and individual therapy (with manualised treatment and matched samples) commences. Complete geographical database commences, with data on all convicted sex offenders in south east London.

1995–2000	Megan's Law (USA, 1996) introduces Community Notification	Rapists are introduced into the group, as well as non-contact offenders (with largely adult victims).
	Sex Offender Act (SOA, 1997) introduces Register of Sex Offenders across England and Wales; the Crime and Disorder Act (1998) introduces Sex Offender Orders	A preliminary review of data suggests that developmental variables – including descriptors of childhood behaviours – is likely to be important in predicting outcomes.
		No marked differences between individual and group therapy is found, although there is some suggestion of greater treatment change in the group modality (Craissati & McClurg, 1997).
2000–05	Criminal Justice Act (CJA, 2003) amends the SOA to include civil Sexual Offender Prevention Orders, and new offences relating to prostitution and exploitation	Analyses of the first 310 contact sexual offenders (139 in treatment) completed. Failure to complete the treatment programme was associated with childhood abuse (emotional, physical or sexual) or problematic childhood behaviours; risk prediction was significantly enhanced by adding a score for the presence of developmental adversity to the Risk Matrix score (Craissati & Beech, 2005)
	More intensive (extended) SOTP including core beliefs and schemas is rolled out across prisons in England and Wales	The programme was amended to exclude low risk, low childhood adversity offenders, with a greater emphasis on inclusion of higher risk psychologically disturbed offenders.
	Publication in UK and USA of new static and dynamic sexual offender risk prediction tools	All offence-specific psychometric measures dropped, given the preponderance of baseline scores within the normal range, and little evidence of change post treatment.

(continued)

Table 1.1 (continued)

Dates	Key events	Challenge Project developments
	Criminal Justice and Court Services Act (2000) sets up Multi-agency Public Protection Arrangement (MAPPA) panels across England and Wales	
2005–10	Adam Walsh Act (USA, 2006) extends Megan's Law to include a national Sex Offender Registration and Notification Act	As the probation service routinely offered interventions to sexual offenders, the Challenge Project increasingly focused on high risk offenders with mental disorder (including personality disorder) and those with previous community or treatment failures. Analysis suggests that violent sexual offenders are not getting into the treatment programme.
	Provision for dangerous offenders in England and Wales to include Indeterminate Sentences for Public Protection (IPP) now implemented (CJA, 2003); abolished in 2012	A longer term follow up (average 9 years at risk) of the original sample. This confirmed the utility of childhood behavioural problems as a proxy for personality disorder in adulthood (Craissati, Webb & Keen, 2008; Craissati, South & Bierer, 2009). Treatment non-completion (36% of the sample) was associated with significantly higher sexual re-offending; a baseline risk score (Risk Matrix + developmental adversity) significantly predicted treatment failure with a two-fold increased likelihood of sexual re-offending with every single increase in score.

	Introduction of the Good Lives Model into an amended relapse prevention programme for prison and probation teams in England and Wales	The programme is amended to improve the treatment completion rate, with particular focus on the baseline risk level. Less emphasis on victim issues and greater emphasis on attachment and relationship dilemmas. Introduction of optional psychiatric support and medication, as well as additional individual support sessions and access to sheltered work project.
2010 –	Introduction of the Child Sex Offender Public Disclosure Scheme (2011) in England and Wales	Analysis of the more recent personality disordered high risk group programme (Craissati & Blundell, 2013) demonstrated a reduced treatment non-completion rate of 25% and encouraging low sexual recidivism rates.
	Introduction of desistance theory into working with sexual offenders, and a move away from addressing cognitive distortions and challenging partial denial	An evaluation of the utility of Locus of Control (LoC) as an indicator of treatment change (McAnena, Craissati & Southgate, 2015) suggested that the treatment group is targeting those sexual offenders with an external LoC and a significant shift towards internal LoC was found post-treatment. The conclusion is that this indicates an increased sense of personal empowerment as a result of treatment; the programme content shifts slightly to include a greater emphasis on service user involvement, and training the offenders to conduct their own evidence based risk assessments.

(continued)

Table 1.1 (continued)

Dates	Key events	Challenge Project developments
	SOTP programmes amend referral criteria to formally exclude low risk sexual offenders	The programme increasingly targeted sexual offenders with a violent, antisocial profile; difficulties emerged with higher levels of recall to prison as a result of rule breaking (but not higher levels of sexual recidivism).

The past twenty-five years

The Challenge Project has been running for over 25 years, and Table 1.1 tracks some of the key decisions that we made as a result of regular ongoing evaluation of the project. Mapped against these changes, the table also sets out some of the key legislative changes and treatment principles that were happening within the broader social and political context of the UK (and to some extent, North America). Mann's (2004) article is very helpful in describing the detailed changes in treatment approach over the years. The aim of this table is not to provide a comprehensive history of sexual offender management over the 25 years, but to highlight the extent to which the subject provokes strong moral, political and social responses. Prior to the 1990s, approaches to managing sexual offenders were largely predicated on treatment, rather than management, with a focus on behavioural modification and social skills training – although psychoanalytic therapy was perhaps more prevalent in the first half of the twentieth century (see Pfafflin, 2016, for a historical overview) – all emphasising an illness model of care. As the Challenge Project commenced in the early 1990s, the prevalent approach to treatment shifted to a focus on cognitive distortions – accepting responsibility, victim empathy, minimisations and justifications – as well as beginning to introduce ideas around intimacy deficits particularly in relation to child sexual abusers. Rather punitive or morally laden ideas within this treatment model were then matched with a decade of legislative change that very significantly enhanced the external controls over sexual offenders: registration, multi-agency public protection arrangements, civil orders, Dangerous Offender sentences, and community notification approaches have been a feature of changes in the UK, but also in North America (albeit adopted at different times). Interestingly, as matters stand currently, treatment developments have moved away from the legislative model of ever more external controls, to emphasise increasingly a strengths based approach that incorporates ideas about lives worth living and protective factors, whilst understanding cognitive distortions as largely shame induced post hoc rationalisations unrelated to risk (Dowsett & Craissati, 2008).

These current ideas – about treatment and about management – are explored in much more detail in Chapters 5 and 6 respectively, with a focus on effective and psychologically informed approaches to reintegrating complex sexual offenders into the community. **Chapter 5** lays out the key ingredients of an evidence-based treatment approach. **Chapter 6** focuses on an examination of the control and risk management approaches of sexual offenders in relation to core psychological and criminological theoretical ideas.

Typologies and theories about sexual offenders

The rest of this book focuses on sexual offenders who can be described as complex – presenting with a combination of relatively high likelihood of sexual recidivism, persistent and pervasive psychological difficulties, and/or deviant sexual interests or perversions. Each of these elements of complexity has its own theoretical underpinning that will be developed within the relevant chapter. For example, Chapter 3 on personality will focus on attachment theory; and Chapter 6 on management will describe desistance theory and the Good Lives Model in detail. However, the task here is to identify and briefly describe some of the key approaches to typologies and sexual offender-specific theories that have had an impact in the past few years, and that are not covered in the subsequent chapters.

There are numerous publications on theoretical ideas relating to sexual offenders; *Theories of Sexual Offending* (Ward, Polaschek & Beech, 2006) is a good example of a book that provides a thorough overview and critique of the various models for the interested reader.

Typologies are essentially classificatory systems that can be either theoretically and clinically derived, or empirically derived; they provide clinical descriptions of the typical features of a group that enable us to distinguish sub-types of offender. They have tremendous utility in signposting important features – a sort of shorthand for the assessor in knowing what to look for in a particular case – and the potential to guide us in terms of wider considerations of future behaviour or of treatment need. However typologies can be frustratingly limited when we try to match the particular idiosyncrasies of the individual sexual offender sitting before us to the general descriptors of the 'type.'

Theoretical models, in contrast to typologies, have the primary task of integrating a systematic set of ideas that have explanatory value – ***why*** something occurred, rather than ***what*** occurred. The challenge for theoretical explanations is to determine their scope – that is, the power of the theoretical ideas to account for a wide range of human behaviours. Is it, for example, possible for a theory of sexual offending to provide a comprehensive explanation of all types of sexual offending (rapists, child sexual abusers and non-contact sexual offenders) or do we require theoretical approaches to account for one aspect of the behaviour such as deviant sexual arousal (Ward *et al.*, 2006).

Child sexual abuser typologies

There are two approaches to the classification of child sexual abusers most commonly encountered in the literature. The first is Cohen, Seghorn and Calmas' (1969) theoretical classification system based on Freud's psychoanalytic ideas of sexual fixation and regression. They propose three types:

1   The **paedophile-fixated** type characterised by emotional immaturity, an inability to sustain enduring adult intimate relationships and an exclusive sexual interest in children.
2   The **paedophile-regressed** type characterised by an ability to maintain adult intimate relationships but who – under situations of particular stress – may revert to the sexual abuse of children.
3   The **paedophile-aggressive** type for whom aggression has become sexualised and gratifying.

Cohen and colleagues' third type – essentially, the sadistic offender – will be discussed in more detail in Chapter 4. Types 1 and 2 remain familiar to us, even though the typology is almost 50 years old. However, we might now understand it as a continuum between two polarised stereotypes: the archetypal paedophile as a loner loitering in parks watching children, offering bribes to children (often but not exclusively boys) for fleeting sexual fondling that is primarily sexually motivated. In contrast, at the other end of the spectrum, the incestuous child sexual abuser who perhaps has only one victim, his pubescent daughter, who is emotionally driven to control and abuse in the context of insecure adult relating and a need to restore self esteem and manage a fear of rejection. The idea of a continuum between these two polarities enables us to consider the individual sexual offender and place him at some point on the continuum, according to the extent to which his presentation and history suggests that his offending is emotionally or sexually driven, and specific to one context or intermittently present according to particular triggers or contexts. Box 1.1 provides very brief (and over simplified) examples of each type.

Box 1.1   Examples of child sexual abuser types

Paedophile offender

Billy has served four previous prison sentences for sexually assaulting boys; he talks of the love he feels for the boys, but now admits that it 'turns to lust.' He wants to stop offending and sees celibacy as the only option open to him.

Incest offender

Mark sexually abused his niece when he was in his mid-forties and she was in her early teens. They became close when her father left home, and her mother asked Mark to babysit when she was out working. Mark was drinking heavily as he was depressed after being made redundant from his work.

Somewhere on the continuum. . .

Stephen is 38 and has sexually offended against girls in the park on two occasions, once when aged 18 and once when 32; both occasions were triggered by a breakdown in stable heterosexual relationships with women his age. He had no idea why he acted as he did, but said that these were impulsive and desperate acts, a 'cry for help.'

The most impressive of the empirically derived typologies for child sexual abusers is Knight and Prentky's (1990) taxonomy (typology). This is primarily a data driven cluster analysis, although influenced by Cohen and colleagues' theoretical model. They propose a model based on two axes, ultimately allowing for 24 different types of offender. Axis I separates offenders into fixated/regressed groups, and high/low social competence; Axis II looks at the meaning of the offence, and considers the amount of contact and the meaning of contact with the victim, the level of physical injury and presence/absence of sadistic features. This is an interesting and worthy approach but, unfortunately, it is seriously limited by the absence of incest offenders within their sample and the very small numbers of offenders that were allocated to some of the less common sub-types.

Rapist typologies

In line with the above typologies, approaches to the classification of rapists has been dominated by two models: Groth's seminal book (1979) in which he proposes three types of rapist, based on a clinical exploration of motives for the offence; and Knight's (1999) empirically derived taxonomy.

Groth restricted his typology to men who rape adult women and focused on their motives and goals within the offence, primarily exploring the different relationships between sexual and emotional drives. His three subtypes can be described as follows:

1   The **anger rapist** is primarily motivated by the need to express rage and hostility, and uses sex as an instrument in achieving this goal; he tends to have intimate relationships characterised by conflict, and harbours feelings of grievance or resentment towards women more widely and the targeted victim (whom he wishes to humiliate); however, the offence may be fairly impulsive, possibly associated with alcohol use, and often triggered by a stressful or humiliating event.

2   The **power rapist** (sometimes referred to as sexual aim rapist) seeks to control and possess the victim and uses sufficient aggression in order to achieve his aim, but violence is not of any particular interest to him; he is likely to struggle with feelings of inadequacy and insecurity, particularly about his 'manhood' and may lead a rather isolated life; the offence is more likely to be premeditated, and sometimes characterised by prior rape fantasies that include 'romantic' or 'seductive' elements.

3   The **sadistic rapist** is the rarest and most dangerous of the subtypes, motivated by a fusion of sexual interest and aggression, deriving his primary sexual pleasure from the infliction of pain or terror on the victim; the offences tend to have idiosyncratic elements, are preceded by considerable planning and the careful selection of a victim, and if repeated, escalate in severity of harm caused.

Interestingly, Groth made no mention of the antisocial type of rapist, a sub group that we would now recognise as the most common type of rapist, probably accounting for up to 50% of sexual offences against adult women, although different sampling methods yield widely differing results. I would therefore suggest that a fourth type – **the antisocial rapist** – needs to be added; these are individuals who rape impulsively and opportunistically, often without evidence of excessive use of force or disturbed sexual interests, who have substantive histories of non-sexual offending (including violent offending) and substance misuse.

Knight (1999) and his colleagues used the same, largely empirical, technique for developing their typology of rapists as they did for child sexual abusers. They arrived at four primary types, based on motivation for the offending and associated characteristics.

1   For the **opportunistic** rapist, the offence is an impulsive act, controlled by situational and contextual factors (including the availability of the victim), and is one of many antisocial behaviours. These offenders can be divided into those with low or high social competence based on the developmental stage at which their high impulsivity was first manifest.

2   The **pervasively angry** type of rapist expresses undifferentiated and generalised anger, with aggression that is expressed towards both men and women. These offenders have long histories of antisocial aggressive behaviour, and can cause their victims high levels of physical injury.

3   The **sexual** type of rapist comprises a more mixed group of offenders in which sadism and social competence may be more or less evident but, for all of whom, there is evidence of enduring sexual preoccupation.

4   The **vindictive** type of rapist commits offences in which anger towards women is their exclusive focus, and the offences tend to contain evidence of a wish to degrade and humiliate the female victim.

Interestingly, although Groth and Knight have approached the development of typologies from different perspectives, they arrive at very similar conclusions. Very simple examples of the four types of rapist are detailed in Box 1.2.

Box 1.2   Examples of rapist types

Martin is an **anger rapist**. His wife left him and took their only child. He brooded on this and wanted revenge in some way. At a party, he chatted to a woman and found out her address. Later that night, he broke into her house and raped her; when she resisted, he punched her repeatedly in the face.

   Seth is a **power rapist**. He was struggling to cope with a new female boss, and colleagues at work teased him about his lack of girlfriend; he spent increasing time alone watching pornography. He started to follow women, and eventually raped

(continued)

(continued)

one, half thinking that she might like him and want to go out with him.

Tim is a **sadistic rapist**. He first started becoming preoccupied with violence, inflicting pain and sexual aggression in adolescence. Initially he robbed women, slapping their breasts, but over time, he became increasingly aggressive, carrying knives, cutting them during the attacks and writing long and sadistically violent stories about murdering women.

Andy is an **antisocial rapist**. He hangs around with a group of career criminals, and has lots of previous convictions for acquisitive crime and drug dealing. One night in the pub, he chatted up a woman, bought her a drink, and she agreed to let him walk her home. At her flat, she said she was tired, but he pushed his way in, raped her, and then left.

Sexual offender-specific theories

As critiqued by Ward and colleagues (2006), sexual offender-specific theories vary in their ability to demonstrate explanatory depth and in their ability to account for the wide range of sexual offending behaviours that they seek to explain. Theorists have tended to focus on either child sexual abusers or on rapists, arguably approaching the former from a psychopathological or psychological perspective and the latter from a more sociological perspective. Here I briefly summarise Finkelhor's model (1984) as being one of the earliest models that continues to be used today, and the one that has been most commonly taught to sexual offenders themselves as part of a psycho-educational approach to treatment. I touch on Marshall and Barbaree's integrated theory (1990) as it is perhaps the theory with the widest reach in terms of encompassing both child sexual abusers and rapists, and it continually adapts and incorporates new learning; and I describe Ward and Siegert's pathways model (2002), as it attempts to draw on the best of prior theories in order to describe the distinct aetiological pathways taken by child sexual abusers. In terms of rapists, the most impressive and empirically based theory is the confluence model of sexual aggression (Buss & Malamuth 1996), which was based on feminist and social learning frameworks, but then incorporated evolutionary analyses of rape. The strength of this last model is partly related to the research that Malamuth and colleagues have undertaken with non-offending men.

Finkelhor's four preconditions model identifies four factors, all of which must be present – indeed, they must occur in temporal sequence, each one necessary for the next one to occur – in order for the sexual abuse of a child to take place. The first precondition is that there must be the motivation to abuse a child sexually and such motivation can be based on either emotional congruence with children, sexual arousal to children and/or blockage (that is, the inability to meet sexual or emotional needs in an adaptive fashion). The second precondition is that of overcoming internal inhibitors to offend; this includes a range of proximal factors such as intoxication, impulsivity, or offence-relevant attitudes and beliefs. The third precondition is that of overcoming external inhibitors or external constraints in order to create opportunities to abuse sexually. This includes opportunities to access the victim, or the absence of protective factors for the child. The fourth precondition is that of overcoming the resistance of the child; this includes resorting to persuasive techniques (such as bribing) as well as verbally and physically threatening techniques, and sexual stimulation.

Marshall and Barbaree's integrated theory of sexual offending is ably and succinctly summarised by Smallbone (2006):

> In short, the model proposes that human males are biologically pre-pared for sexual aggression, that positive psychosocial development generally serves to restrain this potential for sexual aggression, that adverse developmental outcomes interact selectively with negative socio-cultural cues to weaken these restraints, and that sexual offend-ing behaviour itself is precipitated in under-restrained individuals by transitory situational factors such as anger, intoxication and/or opportunity.

There are criticisms of this theory, particularly in terms of the emphasis on loss of control, and its failure to explain satisfactorily the pathway to sexual rather than aggressive offending. Nevertheless, it has had an important role to play in explaining the development, onset and mainte-nance of all types of sexual offending.

Ward and Siegert's pathways model of child sexual abuse pro-poses four clusters of problems that are frequently found in child sexual abusers, and suggests that these problems are manifest in different ways and with different emphasis among the five causal pathways to offend-ing, but all are present in one form or another. These four sets of clinical phenomena include difficulties in identifying and controlling emotional states; social isolation, loneliness and dissatisfaction; offence-supportive cognitions; and deviant sexual fantasies and arousal.

The five pathways are briefly described as follows:

1   Multiple dysfunctional mechanisms, with distorted sexual scripts at the heart of the offender's problems, reflecting early sexualisation experiences and resulting in an idealisation of the adult-child sexual relationship and deviant sexual interests.
2   Deviant sexual scripts comprise a pathway in which early sexualisation may have occurred, but it is expressed not as a fixed deviant sexual interest, but in terms of sex as divorced from intimacy and often mistaken for intimacy.
3   Intimacy deficits is a pathway for offenders with insecure attachment styles but normal sexual scripts who, in certain contexts, are prepared to substitute a child in the place of an adult, and seek a relationship solution to intense loneliness.
4   Emotional dysregulation is the pathway for those offenders who lack emotional competence and control, some of whom may seek sex as a self-soothing strategy or to improve emotional well-being.
5   Antisocial cognitions are those generalists who hold beliefs and attitudes supporting criminal behaviour, and who may hold patriarchal and entitled attitudes, and act in response to opportunities to indulge their sexual urges.

Malamuth's confluence model of sexual aggression (by men perpetrated on women) integrates ideas about why males might have developed particular behavioural tendencies based on evolutionary ideas, with ideas about how these patterns develop across the lifespan. Sexual promiscuity – defined here as a preference for impersonal sex with many partners – is understood as a preferred optimal strategy for males due to evolutionary pressures of natural selection. Hostile masculinity enables men to assert their interests when in direct conflict with those of another, but more specifically, enables men to be capable of using coercion and force to assert their dominance whenever they perceive that a woman may be threatening their reproductive success. This dominance motive operates not only in a sexual context, but in the wider context of controlling female partners, particularly as men – in evolutionary terms – cannot be sure of the paternity of their offspring. The idea is that all men have inherited mechanisms that provide them with a degree of readiness to coerce women sexually; however, differences in childhood developmental experiences (such as parental violence and physical abuse), peer influences (such as self image predicated on the ability to achieve sexual conquests) and cultural (patriarchal) contexts all contribute to whether or not these mechanisms are activated.

Female sexual offenders

Before we conclude this introductory chapter, I want to introduce some limited information on the number of convicted female sexual offenders, and the current thinking on related typologies.

In terms of the Crime Survey in England and Wales (ONS, 2017), female perpetrators were identified in 1% of the overall reports of sexual victimisation experiences and the figures from the Crown Prosecution Service (2017) suggest that a steady rate of 50–60 cases per year where the perpetrator is female have gone to court. However, perhaps of wider interest is the meta-analytic review of Cortoni, Babchishin and Rat (2017): based on 17 samples from 12 countries, they found that around 2% of all recorded sexual crimes are committed by females. This contrasted with the findings from victim surveys that suggested a prevalence rate that was six times higher (12%). The most common group of female perpetrators were adolescents (twice as many as adults). Finally, they found that males were much more likely to self-report victimisation by a female than female victims (40% versus 4%).

In terms of typologies, there is a tendency for practitioners to presume that female perpetrators have co-offended with men, and have been in some way forced into the offending. However, as cited in Cortoni, Babchishin and Rat (2017), although around one third of female perpetrators co-offend (with a male or female), a significant number of these individuals have previously sexually offended alone, or subsequently do so.

Given the small numbers of convicted female offenders, work on typologies has had mixed results, as such offenders appear to comprise a fairly heterogeneous group. For example, Sandler and Freeman (2007) tried to replicate the cluster analysis of Vandiver and Kercher (2004), and they suggested the following classifications:

Criminally limited hebephiles, as the largest cluster, comprising older offenders with a preference for early adolescent victims, with a low likelihood of rearrest, 70% of whose victims were male. These were similar to the idea of nurturers or teacher-lover offenders.

Criminally-prone hebephiles were similar to the above group, except for their much more extensive criminal history, substance misuse, and non-compliance.

Young adult child molesters (or child exploiters) had the youngest offender age and victim age (average four years old); however, in other ways, they were similar to the criminally-limited hebephiles, although they selected male victims only 50% of the time.

High-risk chronic offenders had the highest average number of total arrests, and re-arrests, as well as other criminal behaviours. These offenders were more likely to target female victims (56%) and contained the highest percentage of non-white offenders (38%).

Older non-habitual offenders (average age 39) had the lowest rate of arrest, but served relatively long custodial sentences, having committed crimes against pubescent victims, with no re-arrests.

Homosexual child molesters, as the smallest cluster, targeted mostly female victims (91%), and were similar to the above group, save for the age difference between them (average 44 years) and their victims (five years).

Summary

The models described here are by no means an exhaustive list, but they represent some of the strongest theoretical ideas regarding sexual offending and the explanations as to why and how it occurs. The best

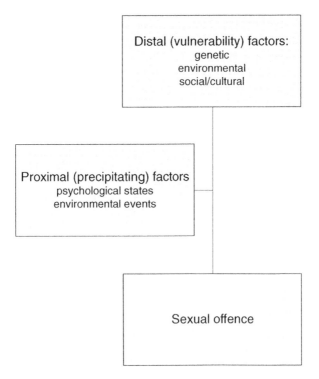

Figure 1.2 A framework for theoretical understanding

of the theories draw, broadly, on the same framework, figuratively represented in Figure 1.2. That is, the theories all draw on distal – or underlying vulnerability – factors that variously emphasise genetic/evolutionary processes, developmental experiences, and social/cultural influences. These can be described as enduring traits that are socially and culturally influenced; they do not predict a sexual offending pathway in a deterministic manner, but can make a person vulnerable to offending sexually when precipitating factors are present. Proximal (precipitating) factors tend to fall into two groups: psychological states interacting with situational events. If we take a very simple example: a drunken rapist – with a childhood experiences of abandonment by his mother – commits his offence on the way home from a night club in which a woman rejected his sexual advances in front of his criminal peer group. The situational event (rejection in front of peers) triggers the psychological state (humiliation and rage, exacerbated by substance misuse) that is particularly salient and unbearable for him in the context of underlying vulnerabilities (that we might hypothesise contain attributions of women as unreliable and rejecting).

This simple framework for understanding – or in psychological terms, formulating – sexual offences, will be returned to throughout the book. It is entirely compatible with the theoretical perspectives detailed in the subsequent chapters on risk, personality and sexually perverse functioning. Arguably, any exploration of the origins and causes of sexual offending needs to take all the features of the framework into account, and to explain the mechanism by which the factors interact to result in a sexual offence being committed.

Note

1 Jimmy Savile was a television and radio celebrity, and a 'household name,' who was knighted in 1990 in honour of his charitable work; after his death in 2011, hundreds of allegations of sexual abuse were made against him, including staff and service users at hospitals where he had been patron.

References

Buss, D.M. and Malamuth, N.M. (eds) (1996). *Sex, Power, Conflict: Evolutionary and Feminist Perspective* (pp. 269–95). New York: Oxford University Press.

Cohen, M.L., Seghorn, T.K. and Calmas, W. (1969). Sociometric study of sex offenders. *Journal of Abnormal Psychology, 74*, 249–55.

Cortoni, F., Babchishin, K. and Rat, C. (2017). The proportion of sexual offenders who are female is higher than thought: A meta-analysis. *Criminal Justice and Behavior, 44*, 145–62.

Craissati, J. and Beech, A. (2005). Risk prediction and failure in a complete urban sample of sex offenders. *Journal of Forensic Psychiatry & Psychology, 16(1)*, 24–50.

Craissati, J. and Blundell, R. (2013). A community service for high-risk mentally disordered sex offenders: A follow-up study. *Journal of Interpersonal Violence, 28(6)*, 1178–200.

Craissati, J. and McClurg, G. (1997). The Challenge Project: A treatment programme evaluation for perpetrators of child sexual abuse. *Child Abuse & Neglect, 21(7)*, 637–48.

Craissati, J., South, R. and Bierer, K. (2009). Exploring the effectiveness of community sex offender treatment in relation to risk and re-offending. *Journal of Forensic Psychiatry & Psychology, 20(6)*, 769–84.

Craissati, J., Webb, L. and Keen, S. (2008). The relationship between developmental variables, personality disorder, and risk in sex offenders. *Sexual Abuse: A Journal of Research and Treatment, 20(2)*, 119–38.

Crown Prosecution Service (2017). *Violence Against Women and Girls Report*. 10th Edition. Ministry of Justice, UK.

Dowsett, J. and Craissati, J. (2008). *Managing Personality Disordered Offenders in the Community: A Psychological Approach*. London: Routledge.

Finkelhor, D. (1984). *Child Sexual Abuse: New Theory and Research*. New York: Free Press.

Groth, N. (1979). *Men Who Rape: The Psychology of the Offender*. US: Springer.

Her Majesty's Inspectorate of Constabulary (2014). *Crime-recording: Making the Victim Count*. (www.justiceinspectorates.gov.uk/hmic).

Home Office (2017). Crime outcomes in England and Wales: Year ending March 2017. 2nd edition. *Statistical Bulletin* HOSB 09/17. London, UK. (www.gov.uk/government/uploads/system/uploads/attachment_data/file/633048/crime-outcomes-hosb0917.pdf).

Knight, R.A. (1999). Validation of a typology for rapists. *Journal of Interpersonal Violence, 14(3)*, 303–30.

Knight, R.A. and Prentky, R.A. (1990). Classifying sexual offenders: The development and corroboration of taxonomic models. In (eds) W.L. Marshall, D.R. Laws and H.E. Barbaree, *Handbook of Sexual Assault: Issues, Theories, and Treatment of the Offender* (pp. 23–52). New York: Plenum Press.

Malamuth, N.M. (1996). The confluence model of sexual aggression: Feminist and evolutionary perspectives. In (eds) D.M. Buss and N.M. Malamuth, *Sex, Power, Conflict: Evolutionary and Feminist Perspective* (pp. 269–95). New York: Oxford University Press.

Mann, R. (2004). Innovations in sex offender treatment. *Journal of Sexual Aggression, 10(2)*, 141–52.

Marshall, W.L. and Barbaree, H.E. (1990). An integrated theory of the etiology of sexual offending. In (eds) W.L. Marshall, D.R. Laws and H.E. Barbaree, *Handbook of Sexual Assault: Issues, Theories, and Treatment of the Offender* (pp. 257–75). New York: Plenum Press.

McAnena, C., Craissati, J. and Southgate, K. (2015). Exploring the role of locus of control in sex offender treatment. *Journal of Sexual Aggression, 22*, 95–106.

Morgan, R. and Kena, G. (2017). *Criminal Victimization 2016*, NCJ251150. US Department of Justice.

Office for National Statistics (2017). *Focus on Violent Crime and Sexual Offences, England and Wales: Year Ending March 2016*. UK: ONS. (www.ons.gov.uk).

Office for National Statistics (2018). *Crime in England and Wales: Year Ending September 2017*. Statistical Bulletin. UK: ONS. (www.ons.gov.uk).

Pfafflin, F. (2016). Psychoanalytic treatment of sex offenders: A short historical sketch. In (ed.) D. Boer, *The Wiley Handbook on the Theories, Assessment and Treatment of Sexual Offending: Volume III* (pp. 1347–54. Chichester: John Wiley & Sons Ltd.

Sandler, J. and Freeman, N. (2007). Typology of female sex offenders: A test of Vandiver and Kercher. *Sexual Abuse: A Journal of Research & Treatment, 19*, 73–89.

Smallbone, S.W. (2006). An attachment-theoretical revision of Marshall and Barbaree's integrated theory of the etiology of sexual offending. In (eds) W.L. Marshall, Y.M. Fernandez, L.E. Marshall and G.A. Serran, *Sexual Offender Treatment: Controversial Issues* (pp. 93–4). West Sussex: John Wiley & Sons Ltd.

Thornton, D. and d'Orazio, D. (2016). Advancing the evolution of sexual offender risk assessment. In (ed.) D. Boer, *The Wiley Handbook on the Theories, Assessment, and Treatment of Sexual Offending. Volume II* (pp. 667–93). Chichester: John Wiley & Sons Ltd.

Tjaden, P. and Thoennes, N. (2006). Extent, nature and consequences of rape victimization: Findings from the *National Violence Against Women Survey*. Washington, DC: U.S. Department of Justice.

Vandiver, D.M. and Kercher, G. (2004). Offender and victim characteristics of registered female sexual offenders in Texas: A proposed typology of female sexual offenders. *Sexual Abuse: A Journal of Research & Treatment, 16*, 121–37.

Ward, T., Polaschek, D. and Beech, A. (2006). *Theories of Sexual Offending*. West Sussex: John Wiley & Sons Ltd.

Ward, T. and Siegert, R.J. (2002). Toward a comprehensive theory of child sexual abuse: A theory knitting perspective. *Psychology, Crime and Law, 9*, 125–43.

2 Risk toolkit

Everything you need to know to make as accurate and defensible a risk assessment as possible

Introduction

A *defensible* risk assessment is one that is considered to be as accurate as possible and that would stand up to scrutiny if challenged; it is an assessment that would be recognised by one's experienced peer group as derived from the current evidence base and reaching justifiable conclusions regarding risk. This is not the same as saying that one's peers would necessarily have come to the same conclusion regarding the level of relative risk and the relevant risky scenarios. All too often, practitioners find themselves – knowingly or unknowingly – resorting to a *defensive* risk assessment. Such an approach tends to be adopted when anxiety about being wrong interferes with one's ability to take a rigorous evidence based approach; it tends to lean towards over-inclusivity, on the common sense basis that more should be better than less (Webster, Haque & Hucker, 2014).

The aim of this chapter is to equip the practitioner with the necessary tools to make quick and accurate assessments of sexual recidivism risk in convicted sexual offenders. It is oriented towards criminal justice, health and social care practitioners predominantly based in the community; after all, the community is where the salient failures really matter on a week to week basis, and it is in the community where practitioners are juggling large caseloads with limited resources and high stakes in terms of professional expectations.

Figure 2.1 nicely outlines the importance of deploying scarce resources in the most productive manner possible. This chapter aims to target the X ('where high producers stop') and to try and avoid the dotted line where effort far outweighs results. Reassuringly, the evidence base in risk assessment supports the premise that the most effective approaches are often the most straightforward.

There is a further reason for marshalling the risk assessment evidence base in a succinct and clear manner, and that relates to the need to argue

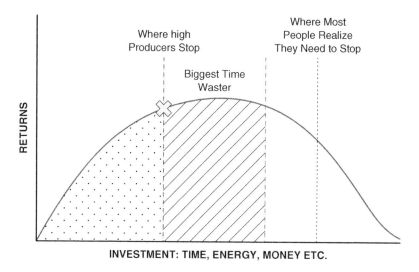

Figure 2.1 The law of diminishing returns in risk assessment (copyright Chris Farmer, www.corporatecoachgroup.com)

a position on risk and an associated management plan in high-stakes environments. Such environments might include giving evidence at a Parole Board panel (England and Wales), post-prison civil commitment hearings (N. America) or holding a different opinion to another professional within the arena of multi-agency public protection arrangements (see Chapter 6 for more details on MAPPA). The ability to put forward a cogent, compelling but accurate argument to support your position is important.

Background to risk assessment tools

The argument against unstructured clinical judgment when risk assessing has been well rehearsed, and the evidence continues to show that such an approach – sometimes referred to as first generation risk assessment – is inferior to subsequent developments. Clinical judgement is the unstructured gathering of information by an appropriately trained professional and leads to a highly individualised assessment of the sexual offender that, unfortunately, has been consistently shown to be inferior to more recent approaches (Bonta & Wormith, 2013).

Second generation risk assessment tools are actuarial and based on static factors – often referred to as historical factors that are unlikely to be subject to change. Such tools are selected from research based on the observed relationship with outcome (that is, sexual recidivism), and explicit rules are provided for combining the items into an overall risk judgement associated with a probability figure (Rettenberger & Craig, 2016). The two actuarial tools most commonly used with sexual offenders are the Static-99 (and its related scales – see http://www.static99.org for more detailed information) and the Risk Matrix 2000. Both tools are described briefly here, although for the interested reader, more detailed information is available in Volume II of the *Wiley Handbook on the Theories, Assessment, and Treatment of Sexual Offending* (ed. Boer, 2016).

Static-99 (Hanson & Thornton, 2000) has been widely researched and is a robust tool with excellent inter-rater reliability and moderate to good predictive accuracy for sexual recidivism and for any (including sexual) violent recidivism. It comprises ten static items that can be organised into four broad categories, and it yields scores that fall into four risk categories associated with relative and absolute risk estimates.

The Risk Matrix 2000 (Thornton, Mann, Webster *et al.*, 2003) – widely used in the UK – comprises two separate scales; one is for measuring the risk of sexual recidivism, the other for measuring violent recidivism risk, and the two scales can be combined into a composite score. The scoring is broken down into two stages, and overall comprises seven items for assessing sexual recidivism and three items for assessing violent recidivism risk. A recently published meta-analysis, Helmus, Babchishin, and Hanson (2013) concluded that all three scales – sexual, violence and combined – provided significant predictive power for the full range of recidivism types, although the sexual scale was most accurate for sexual recidivism.

These second generation risk assessment tools have been criticised in a number of ways: the probability estimates associated with each risk category may not match actual offending rates, particularly in the higher risk categories. Furthermore sexual offenders complain, understandably, that they are weighed down by their histories that cannot change, and statistically based approaches cannot take into account the particular idiosyncrasies of an individual offender, or even a sub group of offenders. Third generation risk assessment tools emerged in an attempt to address these criticisms, and went beyond consideration of risk to take into account needs. These are sometimes referred to as dynamic risk factors, sometimes as criminogenic needs or psychologically meaningful risk factors (Rettenberger & Craig, 2016). Their primary attraction is that they yield richer information in the course of the risk assessment, particularly highlighting features that can guide both interventions aimed at reducing risk, and also the articulation of potentially risky future scenarios.

Structured professional judgement (SPJ) tools tend to be conceptually derived, with reference to the empirical evidence base, but not constrained by any algorithm for scoring or linking the final judgement to empirically derived recidivism probabilities. The most commonly used for sexual offenders was probably the SVR-20 (a 20 item structured professional judgement tool for assessing sexual violence risk, Boer, Hart, Kropp, & Webster, 1997). However, this has now been superseded by the Risk for Sexual Violence Protocol (RSVP: Hart, Kropp, Laws, *et al.*, 2003). The RSVP is essentially a set of guidelines for collecting relevant information about a sexual offender, identifying both the presence of static and dynamic factors, and also their relevance to future sexual recidivism scenarios. It comprises 22 items falling into five domains of functioning. The RSVP is not intended to be a risk prediction tool but a system for formulation and management of male sexual offenders of adult age; however, there is some evidence that the final risk judgement may significantly predict sexual recidivism (Darjee, Russell, Forrest, *et al.*, 2016).

Although currently in vogue, structured professional judgement approaches have been criticised. They are, for example, extremely time consuming to complete, much more so than actuarial scales. Of equal importance, Hanson and Morton-Bourgon's (2009) large review of 118 prediction studies on sexual offenders found that although SPJ (average $r=0.13$) outperformed unstructured judgement ($r=0.05$), it was inferior to purely actuarial instruments ($r=0.25$). This inferior performance in relation to risk prediction may be related to the inclusion of items that are not strongly risk linked in the literature, as well as a lack of guidance as to whether risk concerns should increase, the greater the number of items endorsed. Essentially, the lack of defined criteria for levels of declared risk has the potential to introduce considerable inaccuracies into our risk assessments of sexual offenders.

Before leaving the subject of risk assessment tools, it is worth considering one more instrument – the Stable 2007 (Hanson, Harris, Scott & Helmus, 2007); this could be described as a conceptual actuarial approach, in which the final risk judgement is determined by explicit rules and linked to probability estimates, but the items are selected based on theory or on a combination of theory and empiricism. The Stable 2007 comprises 13 dynamic items, with a total potential score of 26, and research has demonstrated it has good predictive accuracy and incremental predictive power for the prediction of sexual recidivism beyond the Static-99 alone (Hanson, *et al.*, 2007). The tool has now been validated for use in combination with the Risk Matrix 2000, and again was found to yield incremental predictive validity to the Risk Matrix 2000. Structured rules and recidivism estimates can be found in the research paper, Helmus, Hanson, Babchishin and Thornton (2015).

The tool was developed as the result of an interesting project – the Dynamic Supervision Project – which was a prospective longitudinal field trial with probation officers in the community in Canada as the participants. One of the most interesting outcomes was that the combined Static-99/ Stable-2007 risk prediction system showed higher predictive accuracy when used by 'conscientious' officers, who were defined by the fact that they had submitted complete data sets without missing data (Hanson *et al.*, 2007). This raises an important idea, and one that will be emphasised in this chapter: that the quality of a risk assessment is linked to the extent to which the practitioner understands exactly what it is he/she is doing.

Practitioners will need to decide whether to rely exclusively on published risk assessment tools – some of which have been described above – or whether to draw on the evidence base to inform their risk assessments within the policies and procedures adopted by their own organisation. Much depends on the circumstances of the work, and the training and time available. The rest of this chapter details the important principles that should be considered in all cases, and provides guidance when adopting a lean defensible approach.

Precision when risk assessing

What is being assessed?

The first precision rule in risk assessment is to be precise about who is being assessed (a sexual offender) for consideration of which future crime (sexual, violent or general community failure) over what timescale (for example, the duration of a period of treatment or supervision, or over a longer – perhaps indefinite – timescale). To understand the importance of defining what risk is being assessed, consider the vignettes described in Box 2.1. Both Bill and Steve are best risk assessed in relation to three quite different issues: first the likelihood of sexual recidivism, second the potential victim impact if they were to recidivate, and third, the implications should the risk assessment be inaccurate and fail to predict a sexual offence that exposed the practitioner and/or the agency to considerable public scrutiny and criticism. In the case of Steve, he was managed as high risk of harm by the probation service at first, their reasoning having been driven by the concerns around media interest, quite understandably. Steve was enraged at the level of restrictions placed upon him when back in the community, pointing out that a Parole Board panel had explicitly stated that he was sufficiently low risk to be released. He was a prickly and rather litigious individual, and submitted numerous complaints; however, when the risk assessment was broken down into its three separate elements – as detailed in Figure 2.2 – he was somewhat mollified and began to engage more constructively with his probation officer. This demonstrates the importance of working collaboratively and honestly with offenders in negotiating risk ratings; we return to the question of engaging the sexual offender in risk assessment later in this chapter.

Box 2.1 Bill and Steve

Bill raped his step-daughter over a five year period. The trigger for the offences was the breakdown of his relationship with her mother, and the onset of heavy drinking. Having served a ten year prison sentence, he was assessed as a low risk of sexual recidivism on release; however, it was clear that a reoccurrence of child sexual abuse would almost certainly have a devastating psychological impact on any victim. There were no public interest issues in this case.

Steve was released from prison having received an indeterminate sentence for public protection. He had been in and out of prison over the past 20 years, either for theft or for indecent exposure. He posed a high risk of sexual recidivism, but although victims were frightened by his behaviour, the harm was assessed as moderate. However, his last victim happened by chance to be the sister of the local Member of Parliament, and there had been a local but high profile campaign against his release.

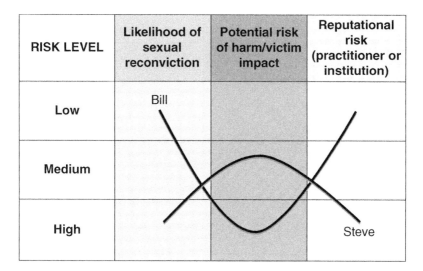

RISK LEVEL	Likelihood of sexual reconviction	Potential risk of harm/victim impact	Reputational risk (practitioner or institution)
Low	Bill		
Medium			
High			Steve

Figure 2.2 Being precise about what type of risk you are talking about

Why base rates matter

The second precision rule in risk assessment is to take note of the relevant base rate; that is, the known proportion of offenders who will reoffend after a specified period of time. This is important for two reasons: first, it anchors the risk assessment in reality, providing a benchmark against which we can compare our own risk assessment. Consider, for example, Table 2.1; this was compiled on the basis of ten diverse studies comprising almost 5,000 sexual offenders (Harris & Hanson, 2004). It can be seen, for example, that although the overall sexual recidivism rate was 14% over five years at risk in the community, only 5% of incest offenders recidivated during this period. It also highlights the fact that sexual offenders are at highest risk during the first five years following release from prison and that, broadly speaking, their risk halves every five years thereafter.

Base rates can be problematic insofar as we know that absolute recidivism rates are changing over time (although relative risk rates have remained static). For example, Friendship and Thornton (2001) found that the sexual recidivism base rate for sexual offenders released from prison in England and Wales halved between 1980 and the early 1990s. Doren (2004) found that average base rates published for the Static-99 had declined from 18% to 13% in newer samples. Further details of falling base rates are detailed in Thornton and d'Orazio (2016), and average around 6% in recent US samples. It is likely that these falling base rates are linked to increasing societal efforts to manage sexual offenders more

Table 2.1 Sexual recidivism rates (adapted from Harris & Hanson, 2004)

	5 years (%)	15 years (%)
Mixed groups of sex offenders	14	24
Victim type		
Adults (rapists)	14	24
Related children (incest offenders)	6	13
Unrelated girls	9	16
Unrelated boys	23	35
Criminal history		
No prior sex offences	10	19
Any prior sex offences	25	37
Age at release		
> 50 years old	7	12
< 50 years old	15	26

aggressively: the increasing length of prison sentences and of time spent under supervision, the intensity of supervision, the quick recourse to recall to prison, and the impact of civil commitment programmes are just some of the reasons put forward (Thornton & d'Orazio, 2016).

The second reason for taking note of base rates is that we know that even the best of risk prediction tools grossly overestimates risk when the base rate is low. In order to demonstrate this effect, Figure 2.3 lays out the calculations for the sexual recidivism rate of incest offenders at risk in the community for five years. So, if we have 100 incest offenders, we would normally expect about five of them to sexually recidivate. Let us say that with our best tool, we have an 80% correct classification rate – this is better than most tools that we have to hand. If you follow the figures in the lighter shade – the re-offenders – you will see that we accurately identify four of the five recidivists (80%) and we accurately identify 76 of the 95 non-recidivists (80%). This means that we missed one of our recidivists – a false negative – and we incorrectly allocated 19 non-recidivists to the recidivist group (false positive). Overall, of the 23 offenders who were assessed as likely to recidivate, only four actually did so (17%) and of the 77 offenders who were assessed as not likely to recidivate, 76 were accurately identified (97%).

What is this telling us? It means that although we were impressively accurate in deciding which incest offenders would not sexually recidivate, we over-estimated sexual risk to the extent that more than 80% of those we thought would sexually recidivate did not actually do so. The implications for these offenders in terms of their human rights – and the resources that are associated with their continued detention – are considerable. As the base rate rises, however, we become significantly more accurate in predicting recidivists, so that our highest risk paedophiles – whose base rate might rise to 25% over five years at risk – can be identified with around 50% accuracy. In a sentence, we are extremely poor at assessing risk in relation to relatively rare events.

Beware of clinical override

The third precision rule in risk assessment is to beware of the temptation to use clinical override, despite the idiosyncrasies of any particular case, except in the most exceptional circumstances. There may, of course, be social or organisational overrides imposed as a result of policy – for example, that all newly released lifers are deemed to be high risk for the first few months of their time in the community – but as detailed above in the first precision rule, it is preferable to be precise about the nature of this 'override.' The evidence is accumulating that professional override

LIFERS   **Base rate of < 5% grave re-offending**
over 5 years at risk in the community
Risk assessment tool with 80%
correct classification rate

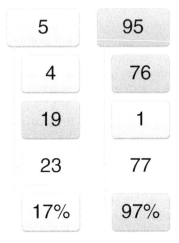

Figure 2.3 Understanding the importance of the base rate for offending

tends to be used increasingly often once 'permission' is given for its use; most importantly, Hanson and Morton-Bourgon's meta-analytic review (2009) found that where research into the effect of professional override was reported, in every study, such adjustments decreased the predictive accuracy of the instruments. The reason for this is not entirely clear, but I would suggest that clinical override provides an opportunity for practitioners to re-insert the features of the case that worry them, and for which the lack of research evidence excluded them from the risk tool.

Understanding the importance and meaning of static factors

If static factors lack meaning and depth, and are by definition unchanging, then why bother with them? I would argue that static factors provide a crucial opportunity to anchor a risk assessment, and propose five good reasons why this should be the first step in a risk assessment.

a) Static tools are simple and quick to complete.
b) Static tools – if completed correctly – provide an accurate measure of relative risk at the group level.

c) Static tools are, unfortunately, more powerful in predicting outcomes than we might wish. For example, the Risk Matrix 2000 has consistently performed better than all other measures in predicting sexual recidivism in the Challenge Project group treatment programme participants; this is despite being able to show a treatment effect in those who have completed the programme. Furthermore, if a score of 1 is added to the Risk Matrix for the presence of either personality disorder, or a history of developmental adversity, then the static risk prediction is further improved (Craissati, Webb & Keen, 2008; Craissati, South & Bierer, 2009).

d) An understanding of the meaning of the static variables yields a wealth of information regarding psychologically meaningful information. Table 2.2 below takes the seven variables of the Risk Matrix 2000/S and highlights the way in which static variables represent a proxy for more dynamic considerations.

e) Perhaps most crucially of all, there is evidence to suggest that forgetting the baseline static risk rating is implicated in serious incident reviews. Examples include Maden's (2006) review of mental health homicides in which he found that a failure to take note of the historical items on the HCR-20 was present in a number of cases; the Rice Review (HMIP, 2006) – an investigation into the homicide committed by a high risk sexual offender whilst managed on probation – also demonstrated the way in which treatment providers may overly rely on compliance and observations regarding progress in treatment, despite the research evidence showing that the clinical impressions of practitioners in this regard are poor risk indicators (Hanson, 2014).

Understanding the key dynamic domains

Table 2.2 clearly identifies the potential overlap between static and dynamic variables, and how, to some extent, the same traits and behaviours are being assessed. Nevertheless, as we have already shown in the section on risk assessment tools (Helmus *et. al.*, 2015), dynamic risk assessments do add – albeit modestly – in an incremental fashion to the accuracy of static risk prediction tools. However, undoubtedly the most helpful element of a dynamic risk assessment is to:

• Explore further whether an individual offender might fall into the sexually recidivating subgroup of the static risk category (for example, whether he is more or less likely to be included in the 25% of highest risk child sexual abusers who offend over five years at risk).

• Develop risk-relevant intervention or management plans, that target the most salient dynamic features.

Table 2.2 Understanding the meaning of static variables (Risk Matrix 2000)

Age at commencement of risk

Sexual drive has strong elements of evolutionary imperative in terms of males peaking in their sexuality around early adulthood; testosterone diminishes thereafter.

However, other offence-related activities diminish over time as well, including antisocial behaviours (largely under control by aged 30) and substance misuse. Offenders report 'feeling tired' of the effects of class A drug use, expressing a desire 'to settle down' and in high risk sexual offenders, a strong wish 'not to die in prison.' Research is now fairly clear that although risk diminishes more slowly with age in sexual offenders than with other types of offender, by age 60 even the highest risk sexual offenders have a negligible recidivism rate (Helmus, Thornton, Hanson & Babchishin, 2012).

Number of appearances at court for sentencing on sexual convictions

Importantly, research tends to suggest that neither the number of victims nor the duration of the abuse influence risk; an offender can engage in a spree of rapes for a period of a year or sexually abuse his daughter for ten years without becoming high risk. The key factor is detection – someone else has to stop them – resulting in the publicly shaming experience of disclosure and conviction. The majority of sexual offenders do not subsequently re-offend, suggesting that some element of this process – being stopped, being shamed or being punished – is sufficient to bring the 'episode' to an end.

Those who sexually re-offend after a previous sexual conviction are therefore driven to overcome the deterrent effect; this includes individuals with a primary or dominant deviant sexual interest, those with significant substance misuse problems and/or those who are highly impulsive. These are the individuals who have strong drives to sexually offend AND who overcome inhibitions to offend.

Number of appearances at court for sentencing on any criminal matters

The greater the number of court appearances for sentencing the more likely it is that a sexual offender has marked antisocial traits; these may include substance misuse, impulsivity and/or an entrenched criminal lifestyle. There seems to be some evidence that an early first conviction (before the age of 13) might be a particularly salient marker for high risk offenders (Loeber, Farrington & Petechuk, 2003).

Of course, it is important to note the age of the offender; for example, ongoing general recidivism past the age of 30 might be an indicator of a more problematic addiction to substances, or more psychopathic features. Remember also, that for those who have numerous general court appearances in their 20s and then a long gap before the commission of a sexual offence, the antisocial history may no longer be a relevant feature of their sexual offending.

Any conviction for a contact sexual offence against a male

This item is really focusing on male child victims, as there is very little known about adult male on male rape, and such offences are rarely included in samples in the risk literature. This item is a marker for greater levels of psychological disturbance in child sexual abusers: research suggests that a very high proportion of such offenders have themselves been sexually abused by adult men when children (Craissati, McClurg & Browne, 2002); they may be more diverse in their sexual interests and orientation, and/or more likely to show a dominant preference for sex with male children, with classical features of the paedophile such as advocating man-boy love.

Any conviction for a contact sexual offence against a stranger

Sexually assaulting a stranger (someone known for less than 24 hours) is a risk indicator because the offender has to overcome a greater range of obstacles in order to offend. He cannot persuade himself that what he is doing is acceptable behaviour or an extension of an intimate relationship in which there is affection. The presence of an attachment relationship or some tenuous connection to the victim is associated with less future risk even though the psychological impact on the victim may be intensely damaging. Stranger attacks are more likely to be associated with high levels of intoxication, or strong emotions that are displaced onto the victim who is representative of an object of hate.

Never having co-habited in an intimate relationship for two or more years

Essentially, in terms of risk, a co-habiting relationship implies one of two things: either a desire in the offender to seek a partner and settle down, or an ability in the offender to be able to attract a 'mate' who is willing to invest emotionally in co-habitation. This is even more important than the actual quality of the relationship, although two years together does imply – perhaps rather tenuously – that the offender has some skills to maintain this relationship adequately.

Those who do not achieve an enduring co-habiting relationship are likely to be hugely avoidant but potentially at opposite ends of the spectrum: there are those who are neither attracted to nor skilled enough to seek an age-appropriate mate, and such individuals tend to be emotionally more attuned to children, perhaps sexually attracted to them. On the other hand, individuals who avoid commitment to a partner – indeed who may experience others being dependent on them as abhorrent – are likely to be highly antisocial, sexually promiscuous and/or unfaithful, perhaps contemptuous in their attitudes to women as partners. They are more likely to view a sexual conquest as an important enhancement of their self image.

(continued)

Table 2.2 (continued)

Any conviction for a non-contact sexual offence

This item is predicated on the assumption that the offender has now committed
a contact sexual offence (it does not apply to those who only have non-
contact sexual convictions). In other words, this is an indicator of escalation
in seriousness in offending. Contrary to expectations, those sexual offenders
who recidivate, tend to do the same thing repeatedly; indeed, there is some
indication that over time, repeat sexual offenders commit less serious crimes
as they age. Therefore, a movement from non-contact to contact sexual
offending is relatively unusual and an indicator of both higher likelihood of
repeat and the possibility of increasing victim harm. It suggests that there
may be something rather unstable in the offender's psychological state; for
example, sadistic sexual offenders are a small group of offenders who may
well have a slightly odd non-contact sexual offence in their background –
such as voyeurism – before commencing an escalating pattern of increasingly
dangerous sexual attacks.

The evidence base consistently points to four broad domains of
dynamic interest (Hanson & Morton-Bourgon, 2005; Mann, Hanson &
Thornton, 2010; Craig, Beech & Cortoni, 2013), and these are shown
in Figure 2.4 below. Thornton and d'Orazio (2016) helpfully refer to
these as long-term vulnerabilities underpinning enduring propensities; these may reoccur even if they are only activated episodically in
response to internal or external triggers. In other words, they should
not be assessed as present as a risk factor simply because they occur
within the context of a single offending episode, but because they are
present over time and in different contexts. Defined in this way, such
vulnerabilities are clearly compatible with an understanding of personality traits that are both persistent and pervasive, issues that we shall
return to in Chapter 3.

Sexual self-regulation incorporates two separate themes. First, the
presence of dominant or exclusive ***deviant sexual interests***; essentially,
a persistent sexual interest in children (pubertal or pre-pubertal), or a
persistent sexual interest in coercive or violent sexual activity, usually
referred to as sadistic sexual interests. The former may be evident as a
result of the history of offending behaviour, and in fact Seto and colleagues (Seto, Sandler &Freeman, 2017) have developed and validated
a simple scale to measure this, called the Revised Screening Scale for
Pedophilic Interests (SSPI-2). The SSPI-2 comprises 5 items: any boy
victim, more than one child victim, any victims under 12, any unrelated

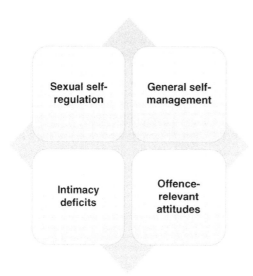

Figure 2.4 Core dynamic risk domains for sexual recidivism

child victim, and arrested for/charged with any child pornography offence. However, remember that paedophilic interests may also become clear in terms of the sexual offender's self report in relation to fantasies and interests. Other, more complex ways of measuring the nature of sexual interest may include phallometry – assessment procedures in which the magnitudes of a man's erectile response to various sexual stimuli is said to reveal his preferences in particular sexual behaviours (Marshall, Hucker, Nitschke & Mokros, 2016).

Sadism is a more controversial term and the subject of dispute in the academic literature; it cannot be inferred from the inevitable aggression that is present in rapists who necessarily coerce and frighten their victims. In order to be accurate – and as a high risk behaviour associated with potential escalation, it is crucial to be specific – as a basic requirement, the infliction of pain, fear and/or humiliation should be closely linked with the achievement of sexual arousal in the offence and in the offence related fantasies.

In relation to both children and adults, there is evidence to suggest that such 'deviance' is not always exclusive or even dominant as a sexual interest. Deviant sexual responses can be evoked by removing constraints to sexual arousal to violence, intoxicating individuals, or by invoking anger towards women (Yates, Barbaree & Marshall, 1984). In other words, there are high risk sexual offenders whose deviant sexual interests fluctuate (as a state rather than a trait) according to the emotional and situational context in which they find themselves.

Sexual preoccupation is the second theme within the domain of sexual self-regulation, and it is often overlooked as assessors focus on deviant sexual interests; nevertheless, it is an important predictor of sexual recidivism. It essentially refers to the central importance that sex may play in regulating an offender's self image and emotional state. In assessing sexual preoccupation, a practitioner should establish whether some of the following features are present:

- An excessive focus on masturbation, either because sexual intercourse is experienced as unsatisfactory, or perhaps because the individual masturbates compulsively. There is no strict definition of compulsivity in this regard, although masturbating more than once a day, or the subjective experience of being unable to curb sexual impulses may offer an indication.
- Seeking out multiple and diverse sexual activity, such as using pornography, prostitutes, or indiscriminate recourse to a range of (legal) sexual partners and types of sexual activity.
- Habitual recourse to sexual fantasies and sexual activity in order to regulate negative emotional states such as loneliness, anger and depression.
- Seeking sexual conquests in order to reassure himself, in the eyes of his male peers, of his masculinity and prowess.

Intimacy deficits focus on the way in which a sexual offender relates to others. In many ways this is best conceptualised as a continuum, on which the two extremes are problematic risk factors: at one end, lies the offender who feels inadequate in relation to other adults and seeks out closeness to children (or vulnerable adults) in order to satisfy emotional needs. This is sometimes referred to as emotional congruence with children, but it may also be present (sometimes referred to as emotional loneliness) when the victim is adult but particularly vulnerable in terms of learning difficulties and emotional immaturity. At the other end of the continuum, lies the offender who avoids emotional commitment, and repeatedly engages in promiscuous sexual encounters, sometimes associated with an aggressive or callous emotional style. Some more suggestions regarding assessment of this domain can be found in Chapter 3 (p. 73).

Deficits in **self-management** are relatively easy to identify but often underestimated in terms of their salience to sexual recidivism, probably because they are so prevalent in higher risk offending populations more widely. This domain includes impulsive and antisocial behaviours including substance misuse, recklessness, rule breaking and emotional volatility; the lack of self-control often results in a chaotic self-defeating criminal lifestyle. Evidence for this domain is largely gathered from the history and accounts of rule-breaking behaviour, although more insightful offenders may well be willing to acknowledge difficulties in this domain as they are not necessarily associated with signs of weakness or 'abnormality' that need to be denied.

The fourth domain – **offence–relevant attitudes** – is probably the most controversial and the weakest domain in relation to risk, and often wrongly assessed. The key evidence based features of this domain include a strong and enduring belief regarding the sexualisation of children (not to be confused with sexual arousal implicit in the commission of a particular offence), and entrenched attitudes regarding entitlement and domination within sexual encounters. There is, in all probability, little difficulty in determining the former characteristic, as the proponent of man-boy/girl love will be unable to contain his impulse to tell you exactly why you are mistaken in disapproving of his 'love interests.' The latter may be a little more difficult to determine, although there will be clues within the sexual offending itself, as well as in the relationship history. Be cautious before assuming that a hostile attitude towards a female practitioner confirms problems in this area; hostility may be as much to do with suspicion regarding authority figures or a dismissive response to a report that reveals other personality traits separate from a specific offence-directed hostility.

The importance of this fourth domain is, perhaps, what should not be included as an aggravating risk feature: denial in all its forms – poor victim empathy, failure to take responsibility for behaviour, minimisations and rationalisations, refusing to engage in treatment, and total denial for complicity in the offence – have all been shown to have no relationship to sexual recidivism. The difficulty that practitioners have in accepting the irrelevance of denial to risk is understandable in emotional and moral terms but problematic in terms of accurate risk assessment and meaningful interventions (Mann *et al.*, 2010). It warrants further consideration, and is discussed in more detail next.

Understanding the function of denial and minimisation

This is a topic that is returned to in Chapters 5 and 6, when we consider treatment and management approaches, but it is important to introduce it here as a misunderstanding about the salience of denial in relation to risk assessment is probably the single most common way in which practitioners can undermine the accuracy of their own risk assessments. The meta-analytic reviews of sexual risk assessment and prediction are clear on this matter; however, we can consider here some additional evidence that may shed light on the psychological meaning of denial (see Dowsett and Craissati, 2008: 111–116 for a more detailed discussion).

Harkins, Beech and Goodwill (2010), when investigating total denial in sexual offenders, found that although low risk offenders (including those with incestuous offences) were higher risk if they were in total denial, higher risk offenders (including those with extra-familial victims) were less likely to recidivate if in total denial than high risk offenders who admitted their offences. This suggests that there may even be something protective about denial in high risk sexual offenders. A subsequent study (Harkins, Howard, Barnett *et al.*, 2015) explored the salience of the risk assessment item 'does not take responsibility for his offence' in the England and Wales offender assessment system used by the probation service. With a sample size of 7,000 sexual offenders, the authors found that not taking responsibility for the offence was associated with significantly lower sexual recidivism. Clinical experience tells us that sexual offenders with stronger links to their social network – including attachments to family and intimate relationships – often maintain total denial of the offence. There is some modest evidence to support this premise – that attachment to others is a healthy and protective trait underpinning denial (Blagden, Winder, Gregson & Thorne, 2011; Craissati, 2015).

Thus, in formulating the mechanism underpinning denial and mini-misation, we need to understand it as a post-hoc rationalisation (Mann *et al.*, 2010) to manage the feelings of shame engendered by exposure as a sexual offender. To develop this idea further, it is perhaps helpful to think of a sexual offender as almost always experiencing feelings of anxiety in the knowledge of his wrongdoing, but exerting considerable energy to maintain this guilty feeling as internal and private. With the exposure that comes with arrest and conviction, these guilty feelings are exposed to the outside world, and with the humiliation and exposure come feelings of shame. It is a natural human response to try and avoid such uncomfortable feelings, and to try and repair our image in the eyes of others; the greater the shame – and there is little greater shame than to be labelled a sexual offender – the greater the attempts to manage our image. To take this formulation to its conclusion, shame is a healthy state of mind as it is linked to both a private acceptance of wrongdoing and also an attachment to others that means we care how we are viewed. Conversely, we can see that those sexual offenders who have a damaged capacity to be aware of their wrongdoing and/or who have failed to forge attachments to others, are therefore more able to acknowledge their behaviour, but they are also more likely to pose a higher risk of sexual recidivism.

'Worry now' (or acute) factors

'Worry now' factors are those acute factors that might indicate a need to intervene immediately, they are the immediate precursors to a sexual re-offence. The most well known and researched approach to these factors is the Acute 2007 (Hanson *et al.*, 2007), which was developed as part of the Dynamic Supervision Project. Although the evidence for linking these factors with sexual recidivism has not been particularly robust or well-established, the seven factors are intuitively helpful, and worth identifying here. They include:

- victim access
- hostility
- sexual preoccupation
- rejection of supervision
- emotional collapse
- collapse of social supports
- substance misuse.

All seven are rated in relation to changes between supervision sessions. That is, they are differentiated from more enduring dynamic factors because the key is to identify a change in the baseline, suggestive of recidivism as potentially imminent. The original research found that all the variables were linked to general recidivism, but only the first four were associated with sexual or violent recidivism; however, the link between recent changes in the factors and subsequent recidivism was not strong.

Although a promising and helpful approach, one of the difficulties with the 'worry now' variables is that sexual offenders tend to hide their deterioration from practitioners once they are en route to sexual re-offending. In our follow up of all Challenge Project participants returned to prison, we repeatedly found offenders to be insightful and open in retrospect – 'I had started to drink more' or 'I was watching more pornography' – but unable to seek help in an honest manner at the time of their deterioration.

Taking an accumulative or an integrative approach?

When using a formal assessment tool such as the Stable 2007, the approach is accumulative in terms of arriving at a final score and risk rating. However, when developing a more descriptive and explanatory account of the risk factors (we return to this idea of 'formulation' in Chapter 3), it may be appropriate to consider risk domains in terms of their interaction; that is, the sum of two factors may be great than each factor considered in isolation.

Box 2.2   Simon and George

Simon was 40 and had a history of participating in paedophile networks, believing absolutely in the sexual nature of young boys. He had three previous sexual convictions of a similar nature, and one of these was committed when drunk. His alcohol use was sporadic but heavy at times. After a long prison sentence, he vowed to maintain sexual abstinence in order to avoid a return to prison. He managed eight years in the community before sexually re-offending; the context was that he was drunk and returning to his flat, when he encountered an adolescent boy begging in the street.

George had numerous previous convictions including armed robberies and two sexual assaults – one with a 13 year old girl, and another with a 46 year old woman. Sex was central to his self image, he was callous and entitled in his attitudes, impulsive and reckless in his behaviours. He had a high score on the Psychopathy Checklist and was open in acknowledging that his sexual offending was opportunistic in the context of boredom, 'I could, so I did'.

It can be seen from Box 2.2 that Simon presented with risk features in both the domains of offence-relevant attitudes and general self-regulation. However, neither risk factor was sufficient in and of itself for a number of years; it was only when the two factors combined and collided with the acute situation of victim access, that an offence reoccurred. Conversely, George presented with marked psychopathic traits that influenced his risk primarily in the domains of sexual self-regulation and general self management, and with a level of risk that was much less context-specific. There is research to show that although psychopathy is not in itself a particularly powerful predictor of sexual recidivism, the combination of dynamic factors with which George presents is a particularly toxic combination, insofar as his psychopathic traits meant that there was little to inhibit him acting impulsively on non-specific opportunities to offend sexually or violently (Porter, ten Brinke & Wilson, 2009).

Another way of conceptualising the way in which different risk variables interact is to consider them in terms of how they influence decision-making (Webster, Haque & Hucker, 2013):

- *Motivators* can be considered as those factors that drive behaviour, increasing the perceived rewards of sexual offending. For example, deviant sexual interests might be a driver for Simon, whilst avoiding boredom by sensation seeking might be the most salient motivating factor for George.
- *Disinhibitors* and *destabilisers* are those factors that remove the impediments to offending, generally because they interfere with an offender's ability to accurately appraise the potential costs of sexually offending. For Simon, alcohol is a clear destabiliser, whereas for George, his impaired capacity for emotional connection with others disinhibits his behaviour.

Protective factors

There is growing interest in the role of protective factors in risk assessment, and indeed a special edition of the journal *Sexual Abuse: A Journal of Research and Treatment* was devoted to the subject (Langton & Worling, 2015). There is also a structured professional judgement tool for the purpose – the Structured Assessment of Protective Factors for Violence Risk (SAPROF) – that has been validated for use with sexual offenders (de Vogel, de Ruiter, Bouman, & de Vries Robbe, 2009). However, research is in its infancy and, conceptually, the area remains confused. For example:

- Are protective factors the opposite end of the spectrum from risk factors (e.g., abstaining from alcohol)?
- Are protective factors independent of risk factors (e.g., a religious belief)?
- Or are protective factors mediating variables (e.g., strong attachment to other mediating the impact of childhood abuse experiences) (de Vries Robbe, Mann, Maruna & Thornton, 2015)?

The SAPROF is a 17-item tool, most of which are dynamic in nature; these are divided into three scales: internal factors, motivational factors, and external factors. Using the SAPROF with sexual offenders – adult and adolescent – the findings are somewhat mixed but encouraging.

Whether or not a formal tool such as the SAPROF is used, a good risk assessment always considers the potential influence of protective factors in the risk summary. However, practitioners should be careful not to assume that common sense variables – such as being in a relationship or being in employment – are automatically protective factors for sexual offenders. Much depends on the circumstances of the original sexual conviction and an understanding of the factors driving risk. For example, if an offender committed their sexual offence in the context of a breakdown in their relationship, then being in a relationship may be an aggravating factor rather than a mitigating factor; however, if the offender had previously engaged in uncommitted and callous sexual encounters but is now settling into a more mature and stable committed relationship, then this indeed may be protective.

Two further words of advice

The importance of previous failures

Although it is implicit in all risk assessment approaches that prior failures should be considered carefully, it is worth making this more explicit here. Many risk management plans fail because insufficient consideration has been given to the nature and speed of prior failures, including non-sexual failures such as recall to prison or dropping out of treatment programmes. Sometimes we can be so concerned about deviant sexual interests, or intimacy deficits, that we fail to identify impulsive rule breaking or emotional volatility as the most immediate concerns, ones that will interfere with our ability to tackle the longer term problems. It is crucial to attend to these prior failures, and to explore with the offender exactly what went wrong on previous occasions. We return to the issue of risk management plans in Chapter 6, but simply emphasise here the need to anticipate the kinds of behaviours that might interfere with resettlement success.

Self-assessment by the sexual offender

Service user involvement (sometimes referred to as 'patient engagement') is now central to many health interventions, and increasingly expected in prisoner populations in the UK (Offender Health Collaborative, 2015).

Indeed, in England and Wales, the National Health Service commissioners have previously expected mentally disordered offenders to be involved in risk management processes. In criminal justice, there is more suspicion about offender involvement in risk assessment, seemingly based on concerns that offender knowledge in this area might enable them to 'fake progress' on dynamic items. The reality is that offenders with significant psychological problems cannot feign sustained progress quite so easily and certainly cannot wipe out their histories of problems in these areas.

There is some evidence to suggest that offenders are, in fact, fairly good assessors of their own and their peers' risk, and that these self-assessments may have something to contribute to the overall risk management plan. For example, Miller (2015) found that self-perceived protective strength was significantly related to self-perceived risk, as well as to sexual recidivism in a sample of sex offenders; Loza, Dhaliwal, Kroner, *et al.*, (2000) asked sexual offenders to complete a Self-Appraisal Questionnaire, and found that not only did the scores relate to eventual recidivism, but the measure performed slightly better than more conventional assessments.

The premise is that involving the offender in his own risk assessment has a significant impact on improving his engagement with the process of abstaining from sexual offending, and in empowering him to understand the features of his behaviour that he should worry about, or at the very least, that others worry about. We return to this idea of empowerment within a desistance model in Chapter 6. However, to illustrate our psycho-educational approach to self assessment within the Challenge Project, Figure 2.5 shows how we help offenders to self assess

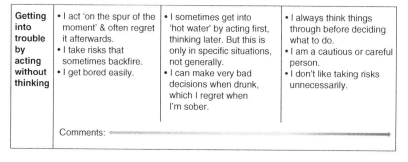

Getting into trouble by acting without thinking	• I act 'on the spur of the moment' & often regret it afterwards. • I take risks that sometimes backfire. • I get bored easily.	• I sometimes get into 'hot water' by acting first, thinking later. But this is only in specific situations, not generally. • I can make very bad decisions when drunk, which I regret when I'm sober.	• I always think things through before deciding what to do. • I am a cautious or careful person. • I don't like taking risks unnecessarily.
Comments:			

Figure 2.5 Service user version of 'poor cognitive problem-solving skills'

along a continuum in relation to the Stable 2007 item 'poor cognitive problem-solving skills.'

Female sexual offenders

Despite the limited range of empirical literature on female sexual offenders, what is available suggests that some of what is discussed in this chapter in relation to risk assessment principles is as relevant to female perpetrators as it is to male perpetrators.

In terms of reconviction rates (base rates), Cortoni, Hanson and Coache's (2010) meta-analytic review of 2,490 female perpetrators, followed up for an average of six and a half years, identified the sexual recidivism rate as less than 3%. Violent recidivism was estimated to be 4% and any general recidivism rates were 19%. The authors point out the dangers of over estimating risk in female sexual offenders, particularly when using actuarial or SPJ approaches that are based on male offenders, none of which have been validated for use with female sexual offenders. They suggest there should be a presumption of low risk, and that the threshold to overrule this should be kept high. Unsurprisingly, the only static factor that appears to be linked to sexual recidivism in females is a prior offence for any type of child abuse. There are no clear indications as to which dynamic risk factors may predict sexual recidivism in females, although substance abuse and antisocial personality traits predict general and violent recidivism (Cortoni & Gannon, 2016).

Summary: decision making 'on the hoof'

This chapter has focused on the salient literature and provided guidance for the busy practitioner. The aim has been to provide an efficient and effective approach to developing good quality and defensible sexual offender risk assessments. Risk assessing 'on the hoof' is not to imply that slapdash approaches suffice in this field, but acknowledges that in the community, managing high risk sexual offenders requires constant vigilance as to the key salient risk indicators from week to week. There is no one right way to risk assess, and organisations differ in their expectations and procedures, as different situations also call for different approaches. Nevertheless, Figure 2.6 summarises five key steps, as outlined in this chapter, that will enable practitioners to be confident and competent in their approach. These steps are then revisited in Chapter 7.

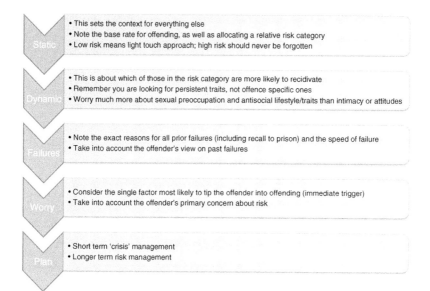

Figure 2.6 Five steps to good risk assessment

References

Blagden, N., Winder, B., Gregson, M. and Thorne, K. (2011). Working with denial in convicted sexual offenders: A qualitative analysis of treatment, professionals' views and experiences, and their implications for practice. *International Journal of Offender Therapy and Comparative Criminology*, 57, 332–56.

Boer, D. (2016). *The Wiley Handbook on the Theories, Assessment and Treatment of Sexual Offending*. Chichester: John Wiley & Sons Ltd.

Boer, D., Hart, S., Kropp, R. and Webster, D. (1997). *Manual for the Sexual Violence Risk-20: Professional Guidelines for Assessing Risk of Sexual Violence*. Vancouver: Mental Health, Law and Policy Institute.

Bonta, J. and Wormith, S. (2013). Applying the risk-need-responsivity principles to offender assessment. In (eds) L. Craig, L. Dixon and T. Gannon, *What Works in Offender Rehabilitation: An Evidence-Based Approach to Assessment and Treatment* (pp. 71–93). Chichester: John Wiley & Sons Ltd.

Cortoni, F. and Gannon, T. (2016). *Assessment of Sexual Offenders*. Chichester: Wiley-Blackwell.

Cortoni, F., Hanson, K. and Coache, M. (2010). The recidivism rates of female sexual offenders are low: A meta-analysis. *Sexual Abuse: A Journal of Research and Treatment*, 22, 387–401.

Craig, L., Beech, A. and Cortoni, F. (2013). What works in assessing risk in sexual and violent offenders. In L. Craig, L. Dixon and T. Gannon (eds), *What Works in Offender Rehabilitation: An Evidence-based Approach to Assessment and Treatment*. Chichester: John Wiley & Sons Ltd.

Craissati, J. (2015). Should we worry about sex offenders who deny their offences? *Probation Journal, 62*, 395–405.

Craissati, J., McClurg, G. and Browne, K. (2002). Characteristics of perpetrators of child sexual abuse who have been sexually victimised as children. *Sexual Abuse: A Journal of Research and Treatment, 14*, 226–38.

Craissati, J., South, R. and Bierer, K. (2009). Exploring the effectiveness of community sex offender treatment in relation to risk and re-offending. *Journal of Forensic Psychiatry & Psychology, 20(6)*, 769–84.

Craissati, J., Webb, L. and Keen, S. (2008). The relationship between developmental variables, personality disorder, and risk in sex offenders. *Sexual Abuse: A Journal of Research and Treatment, 20(2)*, 119–38.

Darjee, R., Russell, K., Forrest, L, Milton, E., Savoie, V., Baron, E., Kirkland, J. and Stobie, S. (2016). Risk for Sexual Violence Protocol (RSVP): A real world study of the reliability, validity and utility of a structured professional judgement instrument in the assessment and management of sexual offenders in South East Scotland. (www.researchgate.net).

De Vogel, V, de Ruiter, C., Bouman, Y. and de Vries Robbe, M. (2009). *SAPROF: Guidelines for the Assessment of Protective Factors for Violence Risk* (English version). Utrecht, The Netherlands: Forum Educatief.

De Vries Robbe, M., Mann, R., Maruna, S. and Thornton, D. (2015). An exploration of protective factors supporting desistance from sexual offending. *Sexual Abuse: A Journal of Research and Treatment, 27*, 16–33.

Doren, D. (2004). Stability of the interpretative risk percentages for the RRASOR and Static-99. *Sexual Abuse: A Journal of Research and Treatment, 16*, 25–36.

Dowsett, J. and Craissati, J. (2008). *Managing Personality Disordered Offenders in the Community: A Psychological Approach*. London: Routledge.

Friendship, C. and Thornton, D. (2001). Sexual reconviction for sexual offenders discharged from prison in England and Wales: Implications for evaluating treatment. *British Journal of Criminology, 41*, 285–92.

Hanson, K. (2014). Sex offenders. In (eds) C.D. Webster, Q. Haque and S.J. Hucker, *Violence Risk-Assessment and Management: Advances Through Structured Professional Judgement and Sequential Redirections* (pp. 148–58). Chichester: John Wiley & Sons Ltd.

Hanson, K., Harris, A., Scott, T. and Helmus, L. (2007). *Assessing the Risk of Sexual Offenders on Community Supervision: The Dynamic Supervision Project*. Corrections Research User Report 2007-05. Ottawa: Public Safety Canada.

Hanson, K. and Morton-Bourgon, K. (2005). The characteristics of persistent sexual offenders: A meta-analysis of recidivism studies. *Journal of Consulting and Clinical Psychology, 73*, 1154–63.

Hanson, K. and Morton-Bourgon, K. (2009). The accuracy of recidivism risk assessments for sexual offenders: A meta-analysis of 118 prediction studies. *Psychological Assessment, 21*, 1–21.

Hanson, K. and Thornton, D. (2000). Improving risk assessment for sex offenders: A comparison of three actuarial scales. *Law and Human Behavior, 24,* 119–36.

Harkins, L, Beech, A. and Goodwill, A. (2010). Examining the influence of denial, motivation, and risk in sexual offenders. *Sexual Abuse: A Journal of Research and Treatment, 22,* 78–94.

Harkins, L., Howard, P., Barnett, G., Wakeling, H. and Miles, C. (2015). Relationships between denial, risk and recidivism in sexual offenders. *Archives Sexual Behavior, 44,* 157–66.

Harris, A. and Hanson, K. (2004). *Sex Offender Recidivism: A Simple Question.* Corrections User Report 2004–03. Ottawa: Public Safety Canada.

Hart, S., Kropp, P.R. and Laws, D.R.; with Klaver, J., Logan, C. and Watt, K.A. (2003). *The Risk for Sexual Violence Protocol (RSVP): Structured Professional Guidelines for Assessing Risk of Sexual Violence.* Vancouver: The Institute Against Family Violence.

Helmus, L., Babchishin, K. and Hanson K. (2013). The predictive accuracy of the Risk Matrix 2000: A meta-analysis. *Sexual Offender Treatment, 8,* 1–24.

Helmus, L., Hanson, K., Babchishin, K. and Thornton, D. (2015). Sex offender risk assessment with the Risk Matrix 2000: Validation and guidelines for combining with the Stable-2007. *Journal of Sexual Aggression,* 21, 136–57.

Helmus, L., Thornton, D., Hanson, R.K. and Babchishin, K.M. (2012). Improving the predictive accuracy of Static-99 and Static-2002 with older sex offenders: Revised age weights. *Sexual Abuse: A Journal of Research and Treatment, 24,* 64–101.

HMIP Inspectorate of Probation (2006). *An Independent Review of a Serious Further Offence Case: Anthony Rice.* London: HMIP.

Langton, C. and Worling, J. (Guest Editors) (2015). Special issue: Protective factors. *Sexual Abuse: A Journal of Research and Treatment, 27,* 1–127.

Loeber, R., Farrington, D. and Petechuk, D. (2003). *Child Delinquency: Early Intervention and Prevention.* Child Delinquency Bulletin Series. US Department of Justice: Office of Juvenile Justice and Delinquency Prevention.

Loza, W., Dhaliwal, G., Kroner, D. and Loza-Fanous, A. (2000). Reliability, construct, and concurrent validities of the self-appraisal questionnaire: A tool for assessing violent and nonviolent recidivism. *Criminal Justice and Behavior,* 27, 356–74.

Maden, A. (2006). *Review of Homicides by Patients with Severe Mental Illness.* National Institute for Mental Health (England), 1–68.

Mann, R., Hanson, K. and Thornton, D. (2010). Assessing risk for sexual recidivism: Some proposals on the nature of psychologically meaningful risk factors. *Sexual Abuse: A Journal of Research and Treatment, 22,* 191–217.

Marshall, W.L., Hucker, S.J., Nitschke, J. and Mokros, A. (2016). Assessment of sexual sadism. In (eds) L.A. Craig and M. Rettenberger, *The Wiley-Blackwell Handbook on the Assessment, Treatment, and Theories of Sexual Offending (Vol. II: Assessment of Sexual Offenders).* Chichester: John Wiley & Sons Ltd.

Miller, H. (2015). Protective strengths, risk, and recidivism in a sample of known sexual offenders. *Sexual Abuse: A Journal of Research and Treatment, 27,* 34–50.

Offender Health Collaborative (2015). *Service User Involvement.* Liaison and Diversion Manager and Practitioner Resources. England and Wales.

Porter, S., ten Brinke, L. and Wilson, K. (2009). Crime profiles and conditional release performance of psychopathic and non-psychopathic sexual offenders. *Legal and Criminological Psychology*, *14*, 109–18.

Rettenberger, M. and Craig, L. (2016) Actuarial risk assessment of sexual offenders. In (ed.) D. Boer, *The Wiley Handbook on the Theories, Assessment, and Treatment of Sexual Offending. Volume II* (pp. 609–41). Chichester: John Wiley & Sons Ltd.

Seto, M., Sandler, J. and Freeman, N. (2017). A revised screening scale for pedophilic interests: predictive and concurrent validity. *Sexual Abuse: A Journal of Research and Treatment*, *29*, 636–57.

Thornton, D., Mann, R., Webster, S., Blud, L., Travers, R., Friendship, C. and Erikson, M. (2003). Distinguishing and combining risks for sexual and violent recidivism. *Annals of the New York Academy of Sciences*, *989*, 225–35.

Thornton, D. and d'Orazio, D. (2016). Advancing the evolution of sexual offender risk assessment. In (ed.) D. Boer, *The Wiley Handbook on the Theories, Assessment, and Treatment of Sexual Offending. Volume II* (pp. 667–93). Chichester, UK: John Wiley & Sons Ltd.

Webster, C., Haque, Q. and Hucker, S. (2013) *Violence Risk-Assessment and Management: Advances Through Structured Professional Judgement and Sequential Redirections*. Chichester: John Wiley & Sons Ltd.

Yates, P., Barbaree, H. and Marshall, W. (1984). Anger and deviant sexual arousal. *Behavior Therapy*, *15*, 287–94.

3   Personality disorder (or pervasive and persistent psychological difficulties)

Why personality matters, and implications for assessing risk and planning interventions

Introduction

In Chapter 2 I covered the first of our three complexities, identifying high risk sexual offenders. In this chapter I turn my attention to the second area of complexity, personality – or strictly speaking – personality disorder. This is a controversial subject, in terms of both the label and also the underlying constructs. In many ways, personality disorder shares many of its controversial features with other mental disorders: the potential to stigmatise individuals, the poor reliability of the diagnosis, the lack of hard science that identifies the underlying construct, and the debate about categorical or continuous approaches. However, I would suggest that personality disorder is associated with two additional characteristics that are inter-related and lie at the heart of its controversial status within forensic mental health in particular. These characteristics are:

- The stigma associated with a judgment of the individual as 'bad not mad' that drives much of the exclusion of such individuals from mainstream mental health services.
- The nature of the disorder is such that the relationship the individual has with the practitioner (and the practitioner's agency) lies at the heart of the diagnosis.

This means that the practitioner is assailed with the full force of the personality disordered individual's dysfunction, and is pushed to act in ways that confirm the individual's understanding of the world as a hostile place. This roller-coaster of thoughts, feelings and behaviour is aggravated by the nature of the offending – odd, violent or disturbing – so that disgust and fear are mingled with irritation and concern.

The aim of this chapter is to try to put the technical arguments about diagnosis to one side, in order to provide a clear model for understanding personality disorder that is useful and accessible to practitioners who are not specialists in the field. A preferred approach is presented here, but I acknowledge that this is not the only possible approach. My premise is that personality disorder is best articulated as a continuum of difficulties, drawing on the terms contained within the classificatory systems, but understanding them as descriptors for the core characteristics (rather as typologies were described in Chapter 1). The current evidence base points strongly to a bio-psycho-social model for explaining the development of personality disorder, and my preference is to place attachment theory at the heart of this understanding.

The chapter will outline the importance of personality disorder in sexual offending, and will focus on an understanding of attachment theory – and the theoretical understanding underpinning therapeutic models in this field – before concluding with a model for formulation with personality disordered sexual offenders.

However, a quick word about terminology in this chapter. I intend to stay with the term personality disorder when referred to the relevant literature and evidence base; however, when referring more broadly to individuals, I prefer to use the term offenders with persistent and pervasive psychological difficulties. As a rather unwieldy phrase, it will be abbreviated to PPPD.

How common is personality disorder in sexual offenders?

Personality disorders are estimated to exist in about 6% of the general population in the UK (Tyrer, Mulder, Crawford, *et al.*, 2010), and they comprise around 20–30% of outpatients presenting to a General Practitioner in primary care. Although there is some variability from study to study, the prevalence rates are broadly comparable in other European countries and North America (see Quirk, Berk, Chanen *et al.*, 2016 for example). The proportions increase when we start to consider patients in secondary mental health care, that is, involved with mental health services (around 30–40%). This latter group are often referred to as having 'co-morbid' personality disorder, meaning that the symptoms co-exist with another mental disorder, for example depression or schizophrenia.

In terms of the prison population, population studies have found personality disorder to be present in excess of 60% of the population; this rate seems to be comparable across the UK and USA (Fazel, S. & Danesh, J, 2002). Of these, around 50% are thought to be dissocial (antisocial), raising questions about the validity of the diagnosis which is so strongly oriented towards offending behaviour. There have been some attempts to measure personality disorder in sexual offenders, although the evidence base is rather out of date. Using the MCMI (a self-report personality questionnaire), studies have found around 60–70% of sexual offenders have elevations on at least one personality disorder scale. Child sexual abusers have tended to report predominately dependent personality traits, some with passive-aggressive features; rapists have tended to show independent personality styles characterised by narcissism and antisocial features (Lehne, 2002). A study using the IPDE (a semi-structured interview approach to the assessment of personality disorder) found the most frequent personality disorder in their sample of sexual offenders to be sadistic, overlapping with antisocial and borderline traits, the latter being particularly prevalent in those with both sexual and violent offending histories (Schroeder, Iffland, Hill *et al.*, 2013). The Challenge Project – at a time when we gathered data on all convicted sexual offenders in the local area – found that 39% of child sexual abusers and 32% of rapists self-reported personality disorder on the MCMI questionnaire; child sexual abusers were significantly more likely to be schizoid or dependent, rapists more likely to be antisocial (Craissati, Webb & Keen, 2008). Table 3.1 later in this chapter provides more descriptive and qualitative information linking PPPD to types of sexual offending behaviour.

Why worry about personality disorder in sexual offenders?

The evidence base shows that there is an inter-dependency between personality disorder, the likelihood of failing or dropping out of statutory requirements, and increased risk of sexual recidivism. To explain further,

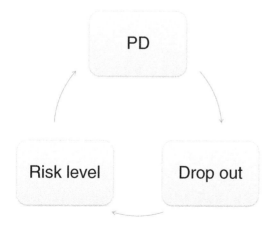

Figure 3.1 The relationship between personality disorder, risk and failure

personality disorder is implicated in both actuarial and structured professional judgement risk assessment tools, indeed it is often double-counted in
terms of the presence of personality disorder and of psychopathy. There is
also fairly robust evidence to suggest that personality traits and behaviours
are significantly associated with the increased likelihood of an offender
failing to complete an order or a programme. These personality-related
characteristics include chaotic lifestyles, poor emotional self-regulation,
impulsive behaviours and substance misuse (summarised in Craissati &
Beech, 2001; Shine & Hobson, 2000; Yu, Geddes & Fazel, 2012).

In practical terms, what does this mean? It means that the personality
disordered sexual offender is more likely than sexual offenders without a
personality disorder to:

- Drop out of treatment
- Be recalled to prison
- Sexually recidivate
- Generally recidivate
- Behave violently
- Disrupt the smooth running of the institution
- Make complaints against staff
- Contribute to staff burnout and sickness
- Die prematurely (Bjorkenstam, Bjorkenstam, Holm *et al.*, 2015)

The label might well be controversial and unhelpful, but the concept –
personality disorder as a proxy term for a cluster of enduring problematic
traits – cannot be ignored as a highly salient consideration when thinking
about complex sexual offenders.

Diagnostic approaches

Having already alluded to some of the controversies regarding the
traditional diagnosis of personality disorder, such as might be found
in the International Classification of Diseases, version 10 (ICD-10,
World Health Organisation, 1992); or in the Diagnostic and Statistical
Manual of Mental Disorders, version 5, (DSM-5, American Psychiatric
Association, 2013), it is important to point out that some offenders find
the label helpful. It can provide them with a sense of 'illness' that is
experienced as compassionate and less blaming, and they sometimes
express a feeling of relief at finally knowing 'what is wrong with me.'
Much, in my view, depends on the sensitivity and transparency with
which the diagnosis is discussed. As has already become apparent in
Chapter 2, there is considerable benefit to offender participation in the

process itself: for example, the benefit of using self-report personality measures such as the MCMI, is not that they are necessarily objectively accurate, but that they emphasise the offender's self-perception, and can therefore be discussed with him as such.

There have also been helpful attempts to try and determine 'severity' within the diagnostic system. This can be thought of as the extent to which the traits are disabling in terms of the individual's life (see below for more detail on this continuum approach). Yang, Coid and Tyrer (2010) adopt a different approach for assessing 'severity,' considering the number of personality disorders present across DSM-IV clusters and within a cluster, with particular weighting given to antisocial personality disorder.

These diagnostic approaches are associated with attempts to achieve a coherent and standardised approach to assessment. There are broadly two approaches:

a) *Semi-structured interviews*

The most commonly used of these tools is the SCID (Structured Clinical Interview for DSM-5 Personality Disorders (First, Williams, Benjamin & Spitzer, 2016)) and the IPDE (International Personality Disorder Examination (Loranger, 1997)). Both these approaches are fairly lengthy to complete, but integrate interview information with background documentation that is based on either ICD-10 or DSM-5 diagnostic criteria. Interestingly, both have screening questionnaires that can be used to identify those who might require the full interview; however, researchers have used the screens as standalone assessment tools (for example, Yang *et al.*, 2010).

b) *Self-report questionnaires*

An example includes the MCMI (Millon Clinical Multiaxial Inventory (Millon, Grossman & Millon, 2015)) which has good validity scales that are able to identify particularly marked tendencies in the respondent to either exaggerate or minimise difficulties. These questionnaires are inevitably distorted by the offender's perception of himself and can only be thought to offer an indication of possible personality disorder, but nevertheless they can yield rich information that is often surprisingly consistent when compared with the outcome of a clinical interview and objective history.

Examples of brief screening questionnaires include the screening version of the IPDE and the SAPAS. The IPDE screening questionnaire comprises 77 self-report items. The SAPAS (Standardised Assessment of Personality – Abbreviated Scale (Moran, Leese, Lee *et al.*, 2003)) has been validated for probation settings, and comprises eight questions. Shaw, Minoudis and Craissati (2012) found that although 40% of a probation sample was identified by the SAPAS as having possible personality disorder, there was little overlap between these cases and those identified via the general probation assessment tool as having marked antisocial traits. This highlights the difficulty of identifying personality problems in those who tend to minimise their difficulties (treatment avoidant) as compared to those with high levels of personal distress (treatment seeking).

Although numerous tools are available, the vast majority of assessments are carried out relying exclusively on a good clinical interview and access to some corroborative information regarding the offender's history. An assessor will be looking at the following areas:

- An absence of emotions
- Frequent mood swings
- Difficulty controlling behaviour
- Hostile attitudes towards others
- Stormy relationships
- High levels of suspiciousness
- Callousness
- Little interest in making friends
- Constantly seeking approval
- Alcohol or substance misuse
- Consistent problems with employment
- Self-harm
- Preoccupation with routine
- Intense emotional outbursts
- Superior attitudes towards others.

Cross referencing this list – not a comprehensive guide but a reasonably detailed one – with the dynamic domains described in Chapter 2, it is easy to see where there may be quite considerable overlap. This is as it should be, given the recommendation that dynamic domains restrict themselves to enduring traits rather than situation specific or offence specific characteristics.

The alternative approach to an illness model using categorical systems of diagnosis is to consider personality in terms of core characteristics falling along a continuum, in which problematic traits are an extension of normal personality functioning. The five-factor model is perhaps the most commonly researched of these models, and an overview of the model can be found in Trull and Widiger (2013). The factors fall on the following dimensions:

1   Neuroticism versus emotional stability
2   Extraversion versus introversion
3   Openness versus closedness to experience
4   Agreeableness versus antagonism
5   Conscientiousness versus undependability.

Alternatively, Tyrer *et al.* (2010) suggest that there may be three dimensions (with some possibility of other dimensions) to personality disorder

1   an externalising potentially aggressive and hostile factor
2   an internalising factor consisting of neurotic, inhibited and avoidant behaviour
3   introversion and social indifference, aloofness and restricted expression of affect.

For the busy practitioner, these various options may not be meaningful, practical or necessary. There is a place for specialist expertise, and for formal diagnosis – most commonly in a legal arena – but for practitioners on the front line, a more clinically meaningful and practically useful approach is required.

At its simplest, personality disorder can usefully be thought of as comprising the three Ps:

- **Psychological** problems that cause distress either to the offender or, more commonly, to others and that are seen as outside the normal range of behaviours in society.
- **Persistent** problems that emerge gradually in adolescence and persist into adulthood, usually evident into the offender's late 20s and 30s, although possibly mellowing in middle age.
- **Pervasive** problems that are evident in terms of thoughts, feelings and behaviour, and that are evident in multiple domains in life (work, relationships, friendships, offending).

One can see how the definition of **psychological** problems is the most inconsistent across cultures and throughout history, subject to fluctuating social norms regarding behaviours. The issue of **persistency** is also not without controversy; we used to think of persistent and pervasive psychological difficulties (PPPD) as fixed and unchanging, not susceptible to intervention. However, the evidence on this has changed, thanks to some prospective long term studies of individuals with either antisocial or borderline personality disorder (see Skodol, Gunderson, Shea *et al.*, 2005 for a summary of the Collaborative Longitudinal Personality Disorders Study [CLPS]).

CLPS found that fewer than half of patients with personality disorder continued to meet full criteria for the diagnosis within two years of their baseline diagnosis; the researchers suggest that there may be two elements to PPPD: first, stable personality traits, that may have normal variants but that in these individuals, are problematically skewed or exaggerated. Second, dysfunctional behaviours, that are attempts to adapt to or compensate for these traits. They propose that it is the latter behaviours that are particularly susceptible to change. Finally, the **pervasive** criterion is important for one key reason – an offender cannot be assumed to have PPPD by reason of his index offence alone, no matter how violent or unusual.

These three Ps are then conceptualised to fall along a continuum, as depicted in Figure 3.2.

It is probable that a formal diagnosis of personality disorder falls somewhere between 'problematic traits in many situations' and 'severe personality problems.' However, the importance of the continuum is to recognise that many individuals with less disabling PPPD perform better in some situations or environments than others. Let us take narcissistic traits as an example: many successful individuals recognise narcissistic traits within themselves that lead to a positive self-image, confident and outgoing social traits, and good leadership skills. However, when these narcissistic traits become more problematic – perhaps the individual lacks insight, or is inflexible and excessively arrogant in his demeanour – then problems in one sphere of life may emerge. For example, an individual may become so competitive and arrogant at work, that he is passed over

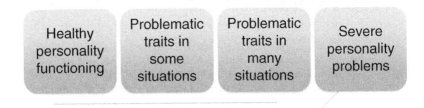

Figure 3.2 A continuum approach to determining PPPD

for promotion and ultimately disciplined; however, at home, in a less competitive climate, and with a non-critical partner, he functions in a more relaxed fashion.

DSM 5 contains ten discrete subtypes of personality disorder, and these terms can be thought of as descriptors for a cluster of core characteristics. As with typologies (Chapter 1) these should be interpreted flexibly and used as a guide for conceptualising problems and communicating with others. I have taken the six types most commonly encountered amongst sexual offenders and provided some descriptive details of the general core characteristics in Table 3.1, as well as some examples of what I consider to be 'typical' or commonly encountered types of sexual offending behaviour, linked to each of the six personality types. This is inevitably a rather over simplistic and mechanistic approach to linking PPPD to sexual offending; later in this chapter, a more individualised formulation-based approach is outlined which provides a more sophisticated understanding of the behaviour.

Psychopathy

Psychopathy – as measured by the Psychopathy Checklist (PCL-R, Hare, 1991) – is thought to be present in about 10–15% of both the UK and American male prison population (Clark, 2000; Conn, Warden, Stuewig *et al.*, 2010) and around 31% of violent male prisoners (Wynn, Hoiseth & Pettersen, 2012). Female offenders have consistently been found to score lower than men on the PCL-R; for example, psychopathy being identified in 11% of violent female prisoners. There may also be gender differences in the expression of psychopathy: men are more likely to be violent, women to self harm; 'manipulative' behaviour may be fraudulent in men and flirtatious in women (see Wynn *et al.*, 2012 for more details on the gender differences in relation to psychopathy).

Psychopathy is an important personality type in offending populations, yet confusingly, it does not appear in the standard classificatory systems. Furthermore, until the more recent revision of the Mental Health Act in England and Wales, psychopathic disorder was one of the categories under which patients could be detained in hospital, but it was not defined in any way that resembled the approach taken by the PCL-R. For the purposes of this book, we refer to psychopathy as measured by the PCL-R. This is a 20-item 'checklist' of factors that are assessed usually on the basis of an interview and access to corroborative background documentation. The 2-factor approach to the PCL-R divides items into those (Factor 1) that

Table 3.1 Personality descriptors, their core characteristics and sexual offender examples

Descriptor (sometimes known as)	Core characteristics	Examples of sexual offender types
Paranoid	Highly mistrusting and suspicious, prone to developing grievances and harbouring resentments; hyper-vigilant to perceived unfairness or slights to which they may over-react. Guarded interpersonally and avoidant of closeness; thinking style is rigid and inflexible.	Generally, sexual offences are not directly associated with paranoid PPPD. • Commits a rape offence within the context of an antisocial lifestyle and peer group; it is only when these traits mature and diminish over the ensuing decade in prison, that problematic paranoid traits begin to emerge. The institutional environment exacerbates the difficulties, impeding progress through the system, even though these traits are not directly linked to risk of sexual recidivism. • Commits a rape offence within the context of sexually promiscuous behaviour associated with a 'partying' lifestyle and considerable Class A drug use. The offence seems rather disinhibited in nature, and on conviction, there is some question of a drug-induced psychotic illness; this settles however, but paranoid traits remain.
Schizoid	Marked emotional detachment, apparent lack of interest in relating to others, inexpressive, and isolated; sometimes there may be a desire to be in a relationship, to be 'normal', but often bewildered by the emotional complexities involved; they often withdraw into engrossing private fantasy lives.	Schizoid sexual offenders tend to fall into two diverse groups: • A single catastrophic offence – involving sexual assault and significant physical violence – is committed, perhaps preceded by a period of infatuation with or harassment of the victim. The perpetrator has no previous convictions and has led an apparently routine – albeit isolated – life, until his encounter with the victim disrupts his equilibrium.

		• Multiple and habitual sexual offending, usually involving relatively low harm activity (non-contact such as child abuse images, indecent exposure). The perpetrator's life is dominated by his involvement in fantasy, often pornography, as a means of relating to others; however, he is less sexually driven or preoccupied than might be supposed, and often prefers to engage in 'collecting and sorting' behaviours linked to his offending.
Dissocial (antisocial)	Tend to view the world as a hostile place where survival is only possible through exploiting others; uninterested in the point of view of others, dismissive of close attachments, and a tendency to dominate within relationships. Impulsive rule breakers.	Antisocial sexual offenders comprise the most common group of rapists. When emotionally unstable traits are also present, then the sexual offences may be more likely to take place within a known relationship. The combined presence of narcissistic traits is indicative of psychopathy. • The perpetrator is committing a burglary whilst intoxicated with alcohol; in the course of the offence, he stumbles across the victim asleep in bed, and impulsively seizes the opportunity to sexually assault her, before running off.
Narcissistic	Overvaluation of self-worth, directing affection to the self and contemptuous of others, holding an expectation that others will recognise and cater to his desires and needs; self-esteem may be brittle, and when the illusion of specialness is challenged, may react with rage.	Narcissistic perpetrators may be responding to what is sometimes called 'a narcissistic wound,' the offending driven by a sense of grievance. However some child sexual offenders have stable narcissistic traits that underpin their promotion of 'man-boy love.'

(continued)

Table 3.1 (continued)

Descriptor (sometimes known as)	Core characteristics	Examples of sexual offender types
		• A known paedophile provokes the police with his intellectual arguments in favour of sexual contact with pubescent boys. He is writing a book on the subject, and has extensive links via the internet with other like-minded offenders.
Emotionally unstable (borderline)	Unstable emotional regulation, including sense of self, moods, interpersonal relationships and behaviours. Intense but rapidly shifting emotions, and a tendency to move from idealisation to denigration of others. Sensitive to perceived criticism and fears of abandonment. May resort to impulsive behaviours (e.g. self harm, substance misuse) to try to regulate distressing feelings.	Sexual offenders with very marked borderline traits tend to have experienced extremely abusive childhoods. Their offending is likely to be either chaotic and/or within the familial context with known victims. • The perpetrator has a long history of inappropriate sexual behaviour in care and subsequently in prison, he is of uncertain or varying sexual orientation, and often homeless and intoxicated. Sexual offences occur in a disorganised manner, often involving relatively minor and disinhibited assaults. • The offending takes place against the partner and the children, the sexual assaults being one component of his more pervasively enmeshed and controlling behaviours, driven most particularly by an overwhelming emotional neediness and terror of abandonment.

Avoidant (anxious)

One of three anxious/fearful disorders; characterised by high levels of social anxiety, feelings of inadequacy and defectiveness. Tend to be shy, awkward, vigilant for signs of rejection/failure, and avoidant of potentially threatening situations. May seek close personal relationships but rely on substance misuse to cope.

Avoidant sexual offenders – part of a cluster of anxious offenders – may be relatively common, particularly in relation to child sexual abusers. However, in terms of the higher risk group, their difficulties may lead to repetitive offending. This group may overlap to some extent with the schizoid group.

- Child sexual offenders who have had aversive dating experiences in adolescence and who find adult intimacy frightening and possibly aversive are likely to seek out children in order to meet their emotional needs. This congruence with children becomes sexualised, often because of their own childhood experiences.
- Some sexual offenders with non-contact offences may want adult intimacy but feel unable to seek it out. They commonly engage well in probation supervision, but may re-offend as it comes to an end, in an attempt – often unconscious – to ensure that the support continues.

denote a callous and selfish personality style, and those (Factor 2) that denote a chronically antisocial lifestyle. A further categorisation is available, with Factor 1 dividing into two facets – interpersonal and affective – and Factor 2 dividing into two facets – lifestyle and antisocial. Although the PCL-R was touched on in Chapter 2 in relation to risk, here it is helpful to consider its relationship to other personality types. In brief, Factor 1 tends to overlap considerably with narcissistic traits, although sometimes offenders with paranoid or schizoid characteristics can also gain elevated scores. Factor 1 has a weak relationship to risk, but can be viewed as the 'treatment interfering' factor; that is, the characteristics that evoke negative responses from practitioners and institutions and that thereby interfere with the offender's ability to progress successfully. Factor 2 can best be understood as requiring a diagnosis of dissocial (antisocial) personality disorder as a necessary – although not always sufficient – component, although emotionally unstable (borderline) traits may also be present. Factor 2 is not only closely linked to risk, but also has the capacity to diminish slightly in severity over time as with the wider literature on maturation in antisocial personality disorder (Skodol *et al.*, 2005). Figure 3.3 shows broadly how one might expect to find psychopathy overlapping proportionally with offending behaviour and antisocial personality disorder.

Rates of psychopathy in sexual offenders are moderately high amongst convicted rapists, although much depends on the sampling method in the study; rates in child sexual offenders tend to be lower than in the general prison population. In our community sample for the Challenge

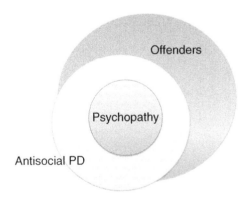

Figure 3.3 Psychopathy in relation to offending and antisocial personality disorder

Project – encompassing all locally convicted sexual offenders – only 2% of child sexual offenders and 3% of rapists met the cut-off for psychopathy (Craissati *et al.*, 2008).

The development of persistent and pervasive personality difficulties

Evolution: why attachment matters

The premise is simple but understanding it is crucial: attachment is the central mechanism by which humans strive to survive a prolonged period of extreme vulnerability until they are sufficiently mature to be independent. Our brains have become primed to seek out others, to bond with key carers, and to ensure that we learn to engage socially, so that we can manage our own and others' states of mind and emotional needs. Ultimately therefore, experiences that threaten the security of our attachment to others, at a fairly subconscious level, threaten our chances of survival. This is why humans engage in such frantic attempts to either deny or to recover from problematic attachments; note how often we work with sexual offenders who refuse to reject an abusive parent, who repeatedly seek out destructive attachments, or who – in their strenuous efforts to deny any need for others – engage in desperately violent controlling ways.

Attachment and sexual offending

Attachment may have its origins and its salience in our evolutionary development and need for survival, but why is it so crucial when thinking about sexual offending? The basic premise here is that sexual offending is essentially a relational act – one instigated and controlled by the perpetrator but enacted between him and the victim; this relationship is best understood in terms of the perpetrator's state of mind and the perpetrator's perception of the victim's state of mind (which may bear no resemblance to his or her actual state of mind). For more information on this and wider discussion of attachment in relation to sexual offending, I suggest reading Craissati, 2012.

To explain further, sometimes the relationship between perpetrator and victim is ***based in reality***. Examples could include the incestuous offender who develops an emotional connection to the victim in whom he sees a version of himself as a child, vulnerable and insecure; this closeness is tainted by his sexualisation of their intimacy. In his mind, his love for the victim is protective, and he interprets her apparent failure to reject him as an indication of her reciprocation of his feelings. An alternative example is the man who, enraged with jealousy and fuelled with alcohol, locks his wife in the house and rapes her repeatedly over the weekend. He needs to reassert his control over her, to punish her for perceived misdemeanours and to prove his dominance in the household; he needs her to feel frightened, regretful and totally in his control, and he seeks small indications – such as her begging him to have permission to go to the toilet – that confirm he has attained his goal.

Perhaps more commonly, the sexual offending contains a relationship between perpetrator and victim that is either symbolic or displaced. **Symbolic relationships** are found when the victim represents a more abstract concept, the most commonly encountered being the stereotypical paedophile and his victim. Such an individual seeks, in his contact with his victim, an attempt to recapture the innocence of the childhood he never had and relates to his victim not as an individual but as 'beautiful and knowing.' In the paedophile's mind, their connection is healing for him, and he knows in his own mind that the boy (for he is not a 'victim' in the paedophile's mind) is blessed by their contact.

Displaced perpetrator-victim relationships are those in which the perpetrator is holding another person in mind when choosing his victim and it is this third person's state of mind that preoccupies him. It is more often encountered in angry, vengeful offenders. Consider, for example, this statement of a sexually abusive step father who said '*in order to get back at her mother, I decided to hurt the only thing that she (the victim's mother) cared about,*' or the enraged rapist who picked a woman from behind who loosely resembled his ex-girlfriend and dragged her down an alleyway, hitting her before pushing her face down ('*so that I didn't have to see her face*') and '*punishing her.*' This latter example is resonant of the angry rapist typology described in Chapter 1 (pp. 18–19).

Summarising the bio-psycho-social model of attachment and personality

To say that the nature-nurture debate is over would perhaps be too provocative and slightly premature. Nevertheless our understanding of attachment, personality development and relevant brain functioning is so much further developed now that we can take much of the heat out of the argument. Helpfully, the findings from psychological theories – such as Mentalisation Based Therapy (Bateman & Fonagy, 2006) are entirely compatible with neuro-physiological advances. Therefore, although I provide some summary narrative under each separate heading below, the reality is that we know there are on-going interactions between the biological and psychological, as each influences the other.

The bio-psycho element

The brain is, of course, infinitely complex, and the views that I summarise here are inevitably simplistic, but they are the facts that I can understand myself, and that I think are helpful for the practitioner in understanding the model. A recommended text for the interested reader – and one from which I have drawn a good deal of this information – is Why Love Matters, (Gerhardt, 2015).

The extent to which personality is understood as being genetically driven is changing over time. It is now accepted that babies have different temperaments: for example, there is a serotonin gene that is associated with greater sensitivity to the social world; babies with the gene are referred to as 'orchids' and without the gene, 'dandelions' (Gerhardt, 2015). Orchids are more susceptible to harsh or neglectful parenting, and therefore more prone to become depressed or antisocial as they develop. Importantly though, orchids may actually flourish more than dandelions in response to very secure parenting; this illustrates the diversity of pathway opportunities within the bio-psycho-social model. Other salient traits may also be biologically driven – for example, inattentiveness and difficulties concentrating, and a propensity for callous and unemotional responses – and around 40% of persistent aggressive behaviour in adulthood can be accounted for by genetics. Overall around 40–50% of personality characteristics more broadly are thought to be genetically driven (Reichborn-Kjennerud, 2010).

The infant, born with these raw materials, then bonds with its adult carers, their task being to help to develop the baby's social capacity by:

- being attuned and responsive to the baby's emotional state
- responding to such non-verbal states with marked contingent mirroring (such as smiling, altered tone of voice, soothing)
- symbolising the child's emotional state accurately in words, and in so doing developing the child's verbal vocabulary that is necessary to manage emotional arousal in a verbal fashion.

With these patterns of interactions endlessly repeated, the child learns to internalise the carers' mirroring responses, and develops a coherent and consistent sense of self; this then enables the child to begin the process of individuation and separation. There are two important consequences of this development: first, the attachment relationship enables the child to learn to manage more negative mood states, with the assistance of verbal capacities; this is achieved by the interaction of rather primitive emotional states (emerging from the amygdala) with more reflective thinking states of mind (in the pre-frontal cortex), so that information can be sifted and sorted, and the most important elements attended to and managed. Second, the child develops a capacity to pick up on the other's state of mind and eventually learns to adjust quickly to the needs of others. This emotional intelligence is developed further in the reflective part of the brain in response to social networks, and builds the capacity to manage emotions and pick up social cues.

Traumatic attachments occur when caregivers are persistently neglectful, intrusive or inconsistent in their caring; this is often due to their own attachment experiences as young children, and their difficulty in processing negative mood states. Problematic attachment experiences are – as stated above – experienced by the child as threatening their survival, and therefore activate first of all the 'fight flight' response, and subsequently, the back-up system for prolonged stress situations – cortisol, the 'stress response.' In short bursts cortisol is adaptive, but with chronic experiences of stress as a result of impaired attachment security, problems emerge with high levels of cortisol being produced in the brain.

• Stress systems become stuck in the 'on' position, and reflective functioning 'gives up trying' to moderate emotional states. This can have the effect of children keeping their emotions close to the surface, focusing closely on their parent's state of mind and making a bid for attention (exaggerating feelings), needing to be needed. It may result in individuals plunging headlong into expressing strong feelings without restraint, with every impulse needing to be gratified, or instil a belief that feelings are overwhelming and dangerous.

• Stress systems can eventually close down and 'switch off' the stress response, adjusting their baseline for being triggered – this is rather like an alcoholic requiring more alcohol before being able to feel intoxicated – leading to a highly avoidant style of managing emotions. For example, boys who are aggressive from an early age are found to have low cortisol levels. Individuals can tend to constrict their emotional responses too quickly, too much and at much lower levels of risk than would normally be the case, and they may exert controlling pressures and fear over their social environment as a means of deflecting intolerable feelings outside of themselves.

In the context of secure attachments, later trauma experiences may be managed without significant longer term effects; the power of an individual's potential to recover seems to be linked to their capacity to find the emotional support they need, and their ability to hold on to their capacity to reflect and process emotional information. Successful processing entails the development of a coherent narrative about the self, with a past, present and future, and this facilitates the laying down of traumatic memories in ways that enable the individual to move on. In the case of unresolved (often called complex) trauma – either early traumatic attachment experiences or subsequent chronic abuse – the level of stress (cortisol) is experienced as overwhelming, and the brain tries every possible means to switch off the arousal, but is no longer assisted by the area of the brain in charge of reflective functioning. Eventually the brain's ability to synthesise information and provide a context and an autobiographical narrative that contains past and future, is impaired. Traumatic memories are fragmented and experienced as present and real rather than past memories.

Adolescence – marked by the onset of puberty – is a particularly salient time in terms of the pathway the individual follows. Developmental vulnerability is not absolutely determined and fixed; adolescence provides a biological opportunity the last significant set of biological changes in the context of surging hormones before adulthood – and a psychological opportunity to repair or aggravate underlying vulnerabilities in relation to attachment and trauma. The core task of adolescence is first and foremost to detach from the primary caregivers and to seek alternative meaningful social bonds with peers, intimate relationships and in the social and cultural institutions of work and education. A combination of factors associated with resilience and successes in social bonds can mitigate against early difficulties. For sexual offenders with PPPD, it is likely that adolescence failed to bring reparative opportunities for early attachment difficulties, and instead such difficulties become aggravated or entrenched. For example, some adolescents seek out an unhealthy identification with a delinquent peer group as an alternative to more pro-social male role models; or alternatively for some, a fragile self esteem may be further crushed by repeated experiences of rejection and humiliation in relation to intimacy. For others, puberty brings with it a physiological (sexual) 'solution' to intolerable feelings of loneliness or uncontained emotional arousal.

Some tips on assessing attachment and trauma

This is not the place for a comprehensive overview of assessment approaches with sexual offenders (see Craissati, 2004 for more detailed guidance), and most practitioners will have experience of taking a psychologically-orientated history that includes some exploration of trauma and loss. However, offenders with marked personality difficulties may be more challenging in their interview responses: for example, highly antisocial individuals may be extremely resistant to talking about their childhood, and almost certainly will want to emphasise the normality of their experiences. For others, their capacity to reflect or to express themselves verbally will be impoverished, and for the more emotionally volatile individuals, intense distress expressed in the interview can unwittingly tend towards avoidance of the key issues.

A few suggestions:

a) If you are able, identify the core personality characteristics in advance, orient your interview towards avoidance of the key areas of resistance, and focus on those aspects most likely to be experienced by the offender as unthreatening (see Chapter 6 for more detail on this approach).

b) Be curious about their world view, rather than imposing your own. This is particularly important when asking about early family relationships, and also when exploring the impact of abuse. That is, you are interested in what the offender thinks, not in whether the offender agrees with what you think!

c) The emotionally intelligent offender who has participated in a reasonable amount of therapy will be able to reflect meaningfully on fairly open questions. For all others, help them out, and beware of the glib use of terms such as 'loving . . . trusting . . . kind' which may be indicative of 'pseudo mentalising.' Try for specific scenarios – one happy memory, one unhappy memory, bed-time rituals, or a time when he was hurt – and explore what happened.

d) Approach questions of childhood physical or sexual abuse cautiously. You will be more likely to elicit key sexual information if you ask 'tell me about your first sexual experience' or 'have you had any early sexual experiences that you now think were a little unusual?'

e) For physical abuse, you may do best if you start with 'were you a naughty child, in trouble quite often?' and edge in from there until you can elicit a sense of whether punishment was excessive or more importantly, unfair.

f) Never accept someone's account of their adult relationships at face value; there is so much potential humiliation at stake, the painful elements are invariably distorted or omitted. Useful avenues of inquiry might include whether someone has ever been in love, or ever been faithful/unfaithful. Who has tended to make the first move in starting and/or ending a relationship; exactly how did the relationship end; how long has the longest relationship been, or how long have you ever been in-between relationships.

The social element of the bio-psycho-social model

Psychologists tend to forget the salience of the social world when focused on their work with individuals, and it is certainly true that there is much less research in this area in relation to personality disorder. However, we know that the social and cultural context determines a good deal of the way in which we interpret traits and behaviours as abnormal or within acceptable limits. Furthermore, it goes without saying that social deprivation – in terms of access to pro-social living and educational environments, as well as quality time interacting with primary carers – will all have a significant impact on shaping emerging problematic personality traits.

Formulation

Formulation is widely used as a term in mental health, but lacks consistency in its definition. In Chapter 2, when pulling together the proposed risk assessment model (Figure 2.6, pp. 50–51), the term 'risk formulation' was not used, although it certainly can be used in that context. My preference is to try and differentiate very clearly the approach to risk assessment – **whether** the offender will recidivate – from the approach to case formulation – **why** the offender behaved as he did.

In the context of this chapter, psychologically-oriented case formulation becomes much more salient. I would propose a definition along the following lines: *case formulation is an organisational framework (usually theoretical) for producing a concise narrative that explains the underlying mechanism of the presenting problem, and proposes hypotheses regarding action to facilitate change.* (Ministry of Justice, 2015). In this chapter we have begun to try to understand higher risk sexual offenders in terms of their developmental trajectory, their emerging PPPDs and the adult patterns of relating that link to serious sexual offending and that may become entrenched and disabling.

On the basis that the more complex the problem, the simpler the solution needs to be, Figure 3.4 provides a simple diagrammatic approach to bringing clarity and order into the formulation. The triangles are influenced by the work of Malan (1995), although amended to incorporate

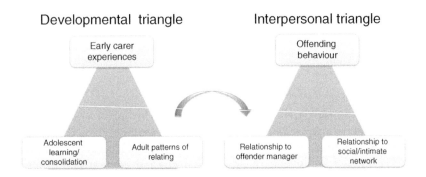

Figure 3.4 Formulating with triangles

key stages/influences in attachment. Thus, the attachment triangle differentiates early attachment influences largely linked to primary carers, from opportunities in adolescence to shape the pathway (for better or worse) that ultimately results in fairly habitual patterns of adult relating. The 'interpersonal triangle' links these adult patterns to the offending behaviour, which – as proposed earlier in this chapter – contains clues to the underlying attachment and trauma experiences. We will return to these triangles in Chapter 6, when thinking about management; at that point, the formulation will need to be developed to anticipate possible dynamics and difficulties in the relationship between the offender and his primary practitioner as well as with the wider network. However, for the moment, let us stay with historical rather than future information, and consider the case of George and Simon in Boxes 3.1 and 3.2 respectively. In a somewhat over simplistic fashion, I have attempted to indicate throughout the narrative where there are bio-psycho-social influences and when there may have been key adolescent turning points or adult patterns evident.

There is no superiority of one theoretical model over another when formulating a case; nor is there one single 'answer' to why the offence happened (Logan, 2017). However, a good formulation should, at the very least,

- be psychologically plausible
- hang together as a causal explanation rather than a list
- highlight and link psychologically salient facts and distil out extraneous information
- create opportunities to envisage 'next steps'
- easy to understand.

It is easy to become passionately embroiled in the debate as to whether the offender should see or agree with the formulation, or whether he should write it or own it. In my view, all options have value and depend on the circumstances: there is only one rule on which I must insist – the formulation is written for the benefit of the recipient, not the writer! It must therefore be written with the recipient in mind: if the formulation is to assist the offender manager, then that practitioner is the recipient; and he/she must be able to understand the narrative as well as find the conclusions helpful and practical; if the formulation is to identify treatment interventions, then the offender needs to understand why and how these link to his past difficulties; and if the formulation is part of a relapse prevention plan, then the offender needs to own it fully, preferably having 'co-produced' it. In other words, the formulation does not represent a single truth, but is a malleable tool that can adapt to circumstances.

So in concluding this chapter, let us consider the case of George and of Simon (Boxes 3.1 and 3.2). We can see immediately, without completing a full risk assessment, that they are likely to be relatively high risk on the basis of historical information: George has a strong antisocial history with a capacity for grievance and entitlement, and Simon seems likely to have considerable problems with sexual self-regulation, as well as with other domains. Previous assessors have identified George as having antisocial personality disorder with paranoid and narcissistic traits, and Simon as having antisocial and borderline personality disorder. This is no surprise, but neither the risk assessment nor the conclusion about personality traits really tells us why they did what they did. A brief formulation – albeit necessarily speculative given the sparse information provided – might provide richer explanatory details.

Box 3.1   George

George was convicted, aged 26, on five counts of rape, the victims being young adult women known to him, and for which he received an indeterminate prison sentence. He has a previous conviction of grievous bodily harm against a rival gang member and convictions for possession of drugs and theft in his adolescence; however, his offending has been more prolific than his list of convictions would suggest *(offence patterns)*.

George's father has apparently served a prison sentence for murder *(bio?)*, although George has not met him and he was never

(continued)

(continued)

referred to by his mother. His mother was a strict but loving parent; however, she worked three jobs to make ends meet *(social)*, and so George was mainly brought up by his loving grandmother who spoilt him and who he adored. At school, George struggled to learn to read and write *(bio)*, and was noticeably inattentive and restless in class *(bio)*. Later, he learnt to cover up his academic deficiencies by becoming the class joker – which ultimately led to him being expelled from school *(psycho – attachment)*.

Tragically, George's grandmother died suddenly when he was aged 11 *(adolescence)*; he returned to live with his mother, and she enlisted the help of her brother – a very strict and religious man – to discipline George. George hid his pain behind anger and rejected all attempts to engage with or control him. He began to hang around with a slightly older delinquent peer group, and his offending behaviour began *(social)*. In retrospect, George identified his state of mind at this time as being one of entitlement – 'I want what they've got' – but he also recognised that he wanted to be accepted by his peers, and he loved the buzz of their lifestyle.

The offences occurred within the context of an antisocial 'party' lifestyle *(social)*, and the victims were women who went to the same night clubs and sometimes dated them. George was a little unclear as to how the sexual offending started, although it was one of the group leaders who instigated the rapes. Nevertheless, he was honest in acknowledging that he needed little encouragement to participate: oral and anal sex was used to express the perpetrators' contempt for and 'ownership' of the victims *(offence pattern)*.

In prison, George initially maintained his denial, not least because his mother stood by him. Ten years passed and his mother became frail and no longer able to visit. George could see his life passing him by, and chose to gradually acknowledge his offending, ultimately participating in a sex offender programme. In some ways George had done well: his regret and shame appeared to be genuine, his infraction of prison rules had reduced greatly, and he had obtained some qualifications and improved his literacy. In other ways, the situation had deteriorated: George was viewed as a prickly, hostile and arrogant man, quick to challenge prison officers, occasionally prone to losing his temper but, more commonly, litigious in his handling of situations. He had a poor relationship with his probation officer in the community and had been turned down for parole on more than one occasion on account of his behaviour *(adult patterns)*.

Box 3.2 Simon

Simon (aged 39) is just about to be released from prison after serving four years of a six year sentence for two counts of indecent assault on two boys (unknown to him) aged 11 and 8. He has two previous court appearances for sexual matters, the first when, aged 19, he was convicted of gross indecency on a seven year old girl, and the second when, aged 26, he was convicted of indecent assault on a 12 year old boy he had been babysitting. He also had convictions for possession of cannabis – he was a heavy marijuana smoker – and an assault on a policeman when he was drunk *(offence patterns)*.

Simon was the eldest child in a large chaotic family. He was very fond of his mother, but she was an alcoholic *(bio?)* who, although loving when sober, was unpredictably aggressive when drunk, and liable to be used sexually by a succession of men, who were sometimes violent to her as well. Simon's father had been around for the first five years of his live, but then left to set up home with another woman, and it was then that the situation deteriorated at home. Simon was a bright child *(bio)*, but failed to progress well at school as he was always preoccupied with concerns about what state the house might be in when he returned and whether or not he would need to go out shoplifting in order to put food on the table *(psycho-attachment)*.

When Simon was 12 *(adolescence)*, he was observed shoplifting by a man who subsequently invited him to his house and gave him some food to take home. Over the period of a few months, Simon was gradually introduced to sexual activity: he was abused by the man he had come to 'love as a father,' and had confused feelings about this *(psycho – trauma)*. Later he was introduced to other men, and it felt good to be able to 'earn a living'; he derived a good deal of satisfaction from the feeling of being desired and thereby 'in control.' During this period, Simon had become close friends with the man's son; this was his first (and probably only) friendship, something that he viewed as special and innocent. Much later in life, Simon could recognise that his offending behaviour was often related to an inarticulate wish to recapture some of the joy of this relationship.

Simon's first conviction occurred within the context of a highly sexualised and promiscuous lifestyle; he was in a relationship with an older woman, but seeking homosexual encounters on a regular basis

(continued)

(continued)

in men's public toilets. The gross indecency occurred impulsively when he came across the girl trying to urinate in the bushes in the park. Thereafter, social services became involved in his family of origin, he was excluded from the household and moved away losing contact with his friend. His later sexual offences were much more planned and he sought out 'handsome lonely boys who thought they knew it all' *(offence pattern)*.

Simon had had numerous contacts with mental health services, usually involving brief admissions to hospital after an act of self harm during a period of emotional distress or broken relationships. In prison, he had set a small fire in his cell in response to a period when he was bullied, and there were numerous allegations of inappropriate sexual advances and/or activity with other prisoners *(adult patterns)*.

George had a relatively secure upbringing for his first decade, although in reality there was a lack of warmth in his bond with his mother that left him feeling anxious, a feeling compounded by his potential humiliation at school when he struggled to perform academically. For this reason, his status as 'special' in the eyes of his grandmother was all the more significant; and the trauma of her death was therefore all the more devastating. This disruption to his attachments came at a crucial point in George's development: he hated the feeling of weakness that came with caring and loss. He therefore rejected dependency on others in favour of an exciting bond with male peers that had elements of the vague glamour associated with his unknown father and that provided an opportunity to substitute status and material acquisitions for intimacy. The sexual offences occurred within this context and represented an opportunity for George to consolidate his self-image in relation to his male peers and to emphasise his ability to 'take' from women rather than to 'need' them.

Simon experienced a very unsettled and abusive childhood in which an affectionate bond with his mother was associated with uncontained states of anxiety and where the unpredictability of life led to a focus on immediate gratification as a means of survival. For Simon, being 'seduced' into an habitually sexually abusive relationship was associated with confusing but largely comforting feelings of being loved and attended to in ways that were predictable and therefore reassuring. For him, the key trauma was not the onset of sexual abuse but the sudden loss of his 'sexual family' – particularly his innocent friendship with the boy – at the point of his first conviction. Subsequent patterns of behaviour were characterised by frantic sexualised contact with others in which he sought to re-capture an idealised version of his childhood, interspersed with brief periods of intense emotional turmoil in which he engaged in dramatic but destructive efforts to try and contain over-whelming feelings of distress.

I must reiterate here that there are a number of models that can be used to underpin the formulation, and which are reflected in the language used; there is also more than one possible formulation, although it is likely that accurate formulations bear considerable similarity to each other in relation to a specific individual. Ideally, these provisional formulations should then integrate the findings from the risk assessment and conclude with some consideration of future management. In order to do this, we will return to George and Simon in Chapter 6.

Summary

A final word about PPPD, attachment theories and sexual offending: there is no one clear pathway to the development of adult psychological difficulties or sexual offending; the interactions between biology, psychological factors and social contexts facilitates the possibility of a myriad of pathways, including – for many – failed opportunities to step away from a developing offending pathway. The key to understanding the link between PPPD and sexual offending is to refrain from imposing our own states of mind on the offender but to retain a sense of curiosity in exploring the sexual offender's state of mind and try to understand it as a series of relational experiences.

References

American Psychiatric Association (2013). *Diagnostic and Statistical Manual of Mental Disorders* 5th edn. Arlington, VA: American Psychiatric Association.

Bateman, A. and Fonagy, P. (2006). *Mentalization-based Treatment for Borderline Personality Disorder: A Practical Guide.* Oxford: Oxford University Press.

Bjorkenstam, E., Bjorkenstam, C., Holm, H., Gerdin, B. and Ekselius, L. (2015). Excess cause-specific mortality in in-patient-treated individuals with personality disorder: 25-year nationwide population-based study. *British Journal of Psychiatry, 207(4)*, 339–45.

Clark, D. (2000). The use of the Hare Psychopathy Checklist Revised to predict offending and institutional misconduct in the English prison system. *Prison Research & Development Bulletin, 9*, 10–14.

Conn, C., Warden, R., Stuewig, J., Kim E., Harty, L. and Hastings, M. (2010). Borderline personality disorder among jail inmates: how common and how distinct? *Correctional Compendium, 35*, 6–13.

Craissati, J. (2004). *Managing High Risk Sex Offenders in the Community: A Psychological Approach.* East Sussex: Brunner-Routledge.

Craissati, J. (2012). Attachment problems and sexual offending. In (eds) A. Beech, L. Craig and K. Browne, *Assessment and Treatment of Sex Offenders: A Handbook* (pp. 13–38). Chichester: John Wiley & Sons Ltd.

Craissati, J. and Beech, A. (2001). Attrition in a community treatment program for child sexual abusers. *Journal of Interpersonal Violence, 16,* 205–21.

Craissati, J., Webb, L. and Keen, S. (2008). The relationship between developmental variables, personality disorder and risk in sex offenders. *Sexual Abuse: A Journal of Research and Treatment, 20,* 119–38.

Fazel, S. and Danesh, J. (2002). Serious mental disorder in 23,000 prisoners: A systematic review of 62 surveys. *The Lancet, 359,* 545–48.

First, M., Williams, J., Benjamin, L. and Spitzer, R. (2016). *Structured Clinical Interview for DSM-5 Personality Disorders (SCID-5-PD).* Arlington, VA: American Psychiatric Association.

Gerhardt, S. (2015). *Why Love Matters: How Affection Shapes a Baby's Brain.* East Sussex: Routledge.

Hare, R. (1991). *Manual for the Revised Psychopathy Checklist.* Toronto: Multi-Health Systems.

Lehne, G. (2002). The Neo-PI and the MCMI in the forensic evaluation of sex offenders. In (eds) P. Costa and T. Widiger, *Personality Disorders and the Five-Factor Model of Personality* (pp. 175–88). Washington, DC: American Psychological Association.

Logan, C. (2017). Formulation for Forensic Practitioners. In (eds) R. Roesch and A. Cook, *Handbook of Forensic Mental Health Services* (pp. 153–78). Abingdon: Routledge.

Loranger, A.M. (1997). International Personality Disorder Examination (IPDE). In (eds) A.M. Loranger, A. Janca and N. Sartorius, *Assessment and Diagnosis of Personality Disorders. The ICD-10 International Personality Disorder Examination (IPDE)* (pp. 43–51). Cambridge: Cambridge University Press.

Malan, D. (1995). *Individual Psychotherapy and the Science of Psychodynamics.* Florida: Taylor & Francis.

Millon, T., Grossman, S. and Millon, C. (2015). *Millon Clinical Multiaxial Inventory-IV.* Oxford: Pearson, PsychCorp.

Ministry of Justice (2015). *Working with Personality Disordered Offenders: A Practitioners Guide.* UK: National Offender Management Service.

Moran, P., Leese, M., Lee, T., Walters, P., Thornicroft, G. and Mann, A. (2003). Standardised Assessment of Personality – Abbreviated Scale (SAPAS): preliminary validation of a brief screen for personality disorder. *British Journal of Psychiatry, 183,* 228–323.

Quirk, S., Berk, M., Chanen, A., Koivumaa-Honkanen, H., Brennan-Olsen, S., Pasco, J. and Williams, L. (2016). Population prevalence of personality disorder and associations with physical health comorbidities and health care service utilization: A review. *Personality Disorders: Theory, Research, & Treatment, 7,* 136–46.

Reichborn-Kjennerud, T. (2010). The genetic epidemiology of personality disorders. *Dialogues Clinical Neuroscience, 12 (1)*, 103–14.

Schroeder, M., Iffland, J., Hill, A., Berner, W. and Briken, P. (2013). Personality disorders in men with sexual and violent criminal offense histories. *Journal of Personality Disorders, 27*, 519–30.

Shaw, J., Minoudis, P. and Craissati, J. (2012). A comparison of the standardised assessment of personality – abbreviated scale and the offender assessment system personality disorder screen in a probation community sample. *The Journal of Forensic Psychiatry & Psychology*, 1–12.

Shine, J. and Hobson, J. (2000). Institutional behaviour and time in treatment among psychopaths admitted to a prison-based therapeutic community. *Medicine, Science & Law, 40*, 327–35.

Skodol, A., Gunderson, J., Shea, M., McGlashan, T., Morey, L., Sanislow, C., Bender, D., Grilo, C., Aznarini, M., Yen, S., Pagano, M. and Stout, R. (2005). The collaborative longitudinal personality disorders study (CLPS): Overview and implications. *Journal of Personality Disorder, 19*, 487–504.

Trull, T. and Widiger, T. (2013). Dimensional models of personality: The five-factor model and the DSM-5. *Dialogues in Clinical Neuroscience, 15*, 135–46.

Tyrer, P., Mulder, R., Crawford, M., Newton-Howes, G., Simonsen, E., Ndetei, D., Koldobsky, N., Fossati, A., Mbatia, J. and Barrett, B. (2010). Personality Disorder: a new global perspective. *World Psychiatry, 9*, 56–60.

World Health Organisation (1992). *International Classification of Diseases: Version 10.* Geneva: WHO.

Wynn, R., Hoiseth, M. and Petersen, G. (2012). Psychopathy in women: Theoretical and clinical perspectives. *International Journal of Women's Health, 4*, 257–63.

Yang, M., Coid, J. and Tyrer, P. (2010). Personality pathology recorded by severity: National survey. *The British Journal of Psychiatry, 197*, 193–99.

Yu, R., Geddes, J. and Fazel, S. (2012). Personality disorders, violence and antisocial behavior: A systematic review and meta-regression analysis. *Journal of Personality Disorders, 26*, 775–92.

4 Perversion: the sexualisation of aggression

Making the case for resurrecting unfashionable psychoanalytic ideas to understand complex presentations

Introduction

Psychoanalysis – the psychological and therapeutic model that dominated for much of the twentieth century, until the development of behavioural approaches in the 1970s – has fallen out of favour over the past 40 years. As a stark reminder of this, in the recent publication of an enormous and specialist sex offender handbook (Ed. Boer, 2016) only one of around 80 chapters is devoted to the psychoanalytical approach. There are undoubtedly a number of reasons for this, including the elitist connotations associated with the expensive training and predominantly private practice involved with psychoanalysis. At a clinical level, the treatment model has often been thought to be inappropriate for sexual offenders – and other offenders – due to the level of psychological disturbance. Perhaps most importantly – and a lesson for us all – is the psychoanalysts' failure to adopt an explicitly research oriented approach towards establishing their model as making an effective contribution to the treatment evaluation literature (Pfafflin, 2016). Their rather insular approach is exacerbated by an unfortunate tendency to write about complicated ideas in complicated language.

Having highlighted a number of criticisms, there are of course a number of positive reasons to consider psychoanalysis as having made a substantial contribution, if not to the treatment, then certainly to our understanding of sexual offending. First and foremost we tend to forget that many of the ideas that we use routinely as criminal justice practitioners are derived from psychoanalysis; we have reintroduced ideas around the 'therapist-patient' relationship in the delivery of sex offender treatment programmes, even though we almost never reference 'transference,' and we use the term 'splitting' when working with personality disorder without having read one word of Sigmund Freud, let alone his work on Fetishism (1927). Furthermore, although we have already identified Bowlby – the 'father' of attachment ideas – as a psychoanalyst, some of the most widely followed therapies – Beck's cognitive therapy (1975) or Mentalisation Based Therapy (Bateman & Fonagy, 2006) have been developed by psychoanalytically trained practitioners.

Invaluable work has been achieved by the few specialist forensic psychoanalytic clinics; in the UK, the Portman Clinic[1] has been at the centre of theoretical developments in relation to a psychoanalytical understanding of sexual offending. The aim of this chapter is to highlight three particular areas in which psychoanalytic ideas are, in my view, particularly significant in enriching our understanding; that is, helping us to make sense of the apparently incomprehensible.

These three areas are as follows:

- **Identification with the aggressor**
  Understanding the mechanism that links childhood sexual victimisation to adult sexual offending, often despite the best intentions of the traumatised perpetrator, only to be endlessly repeated.
- **Perversion and the core complex**
  Getting to grips with an explanation of the sexualisation of aggression that provides us with a new way of thinking about deviant sexual interests and paraphilias.
- **Fantasy as a regulator of self-esteem – practical applications**
  Broadening our understanding of fantasy – its nature and role – and how it may relate to sexual offending, in order to better conceptualise and work with the reported experiences of sexual offenders.

In each of these areas, I bring a non-psychoanalytic interpretation of the psychoanalytic ideas. I am not fully trained in the model, just an interested amateur; but it seems to me that there is ample scope for all practitioners to benefit from an understanding of the concepts. As with attachment theory, the science and mechanisms that underpin the construct can be understood at a sophisticated and specialist level, or in more descriptive terms that have face validity for the average practitioner. I make no apology for this simplification of the ideas, if it makes them more accessible.

Identification with the aggressor

Sometimes a sexual offender, abused in childhood, will say in therapy, 'why did I do it . . . it was so horrible when I was a child, I vowed I would never do any such thing to someone else, and yet here we are . . . somehow it just happened and I didn't seem to be able to stop myself' (here the offending is ego dystonic – in conflict with one's self image). For others, the offending may be ego syntonic (in harmony with one's self image), and the childhood sexual victimisation idealised.

In Chapter 2, when discussing the trauma of childhood sexual abuse, I touched on our findings from working with sexual offenders on the Challenge Project. Just to recap the salient points here: our research showed that the sexually abused perpetrators had never successfully disclosed their abuse as a child (Craissati, McClurg & Browne, 2002). Furthermore, it seemed that the key elements of the trauma lay not in the sexual act itself, but in the subsequent attempts to make sense of the experience, with two post hoc beliefs commonly held by sexually abused offenders:

- intense feelings of anxiety at having been 'chosen' and interpreting this to mean that he may be homosexual in orientation (or at least, be perceived as such by others)
- struggling to understand why he was physically aroused during the abuse and interpreting this to mean that he was culpable.

Identification with the aggressor was first discussed in relation to trauma by Ferenczi but taken up and developed by Anna Freud in her book, *The Ego and the Mechanisms of Defence* (A. Freud, 1993, originally published in 1936). Miller (1998) helpfully summarises the theory, and provides case material as examples. She points out that in the face of any trauma as a child, the single most important factor in helping the child to manage and assimilate such experiences is the presence of an adult who can identify with the child's point of view without being overwhelmed by the experience. In the absence of such an adult – and in the context, for example, of chronic sexual victimisation – the child is unable to master the experience and is overwhelmed with feelings of confusion and helplessness. The situation is made all the more confusing and unmanageable when highly conflicted feelings – love/hate, pleasure/pain – are involved.

These unmanaged and unprocessed experiences lead to two related responses:

- First, anxiety drives the individual to make repeated attempts at mastery – the 'compulsion to repeat' – in which the goal (mastery of the trauma) involves repetition until another 'ending' can be sought in which the trauma is somehow resolved, perhaps by the role of victim being exchanged for that of the aggressor.

- Second, the terrible feelings of helplessness, humiliation or fear need to be disowned in order to be survived, split off and projected into others; then by identifying with the aggressor, the individual tackles and stamps out these intolerable feelings of weakness by scapegoating the victim.

Box 4.1   Gary

Gary (aged 43) was a high-risk paedophile with multiple male victims. He had engaged in considerable amounts of cognitive behavioural sex offender programme work, with good effect. As a child he had been reared in an all female household, and sexually abused by a teenage female cousin when young; the abuse had been painful, physically and emotionally, and he was conscious of anger towards his cousin as well as having later rejected ideas of intimacy with women. However, he had remained extremely resistant to acknowledging that his later sexual victimisation by a male teacher at school had also been abusive. The reality was that he had been targeted, abused over a three-year period, used to recruit younger boys and then dropped by the teacher at puberty with the excuse 'other boys need my support now, and you can move on and find your own relationships.'

Extracts from conversations with Gary:

Gary's own victimisation by the teacher

'. . . we had a great relationship, yes, he was the male role model that I needed, but I also knew I was loved by him . . . we had so much in common . . . It came to an end, these things do, there was no big rejection . . . he just let me go gently . . . feel angry with him? No, how could I? If I start to hate him, then I have to hate myself, because I'm just like him . . . I followed his script so exactly it's weird when I think about it (referring to his offending).

Gary's offending

'. . . at the time you have to believe it's love, I couldn't have done it otherwise . . . yes it turns to lust over time . . . but at first it's absolute heaven, bliss, it seems like we have a perfect understanding . . . it's only later that anxiety . . . doubts . . . start to spoil it . . .'

Box 4.1 highlights the case of Gary, and provides some summarised extracts of conversations with him in therapy. Identification with the aggressor was a very helpful concept in trying to understand Gary's reluctance to label himself as an abused boy; we came to understand the trauma as centring on the intolerable experience of being rejected by the teacher, which raised overwhelming anxieties as to whether Gary had actually ever been loved, or simply deceived? He had compulsively assumed the role of 'loving' teacher with his own victims, both in a desperate attempt to reassure himself that he was loved and also in an attempt to reverse the feelings of helplessness at being abandoned. Clearly, in the therapeutic relationship, there was no direct discussion of identification of the aggressor or repetition compulsion; it is not usually helpful to use these technical terms in the clinical work, but rather, to show the person how these mechanisms work in them. Understanding more about the nature of the trauma and its link to his offending enabled Gary, over time, to feel more in control of his childhood experiences and less driven by some unnamed anxiety.

Perversion and the core complex

Perversion is an out-dated and potentially derogatory term, but nevertheless one that has specific and clinically meaningful connotations in the psychoanalytic literature. Its definition in the Oxford English Dictionary is 'distortion or corruption of the original course, meaning, or state of something' (https://en.oxforddictionaries.com/definition/perversion). In its original, and strictest clinical sense, it is used specifically to denote the sexualisation of the aggressive instinct; that is, a repetitive and relatively fixed behaviour – a sexual act which is insistent and gratifying – that leads potentially to orgasm. A succinct overview of the history of psychoanalytic approaches to perversion can be found in Yakeley (2010, Chapter 4, 56–67). In this section, I concentrate primarily on one theoretical perspective (the core complex), but before outlining this model in detail, it is useful to refer to two helpful precursors.

Stoller (1975) referred to perversions as the 'erotic form of hatred,' and he was one of the first to think about not just identifying the behaviours, but exploring the motivations that might lie behind them. He introduced the idea of perverse sexual scripts as a solution to a common dilemma – as boys strive for masculinity and individuation and separation from their mothers they may be made to feel humiliated or emasculated. In Stoller's view, behaviours such as cross-dressing apparently re-enact the trauma, in which the boy or man is emasculated, but actually he triumphs, because he then masturbates and ejaculates, re-asserting his masculinity. For Stoller, the perverse fantasy or act acquired its gratificatory powers through its capacity to reverse childhood-induced psychological traumas in a symbolic act of revenge: where once the individual was 'victim' he was now victor,' triumphing over the people who had humiliated him in his mind. This idea resonates with the above section on identification with the aggressor. Rosen (1979) then developed these ideas, with the focus on perversion as a regulator of self-esteem. He took the view that stable and positive self-esteem is central to an integrated personality (sense of self in relation to others); thus a poor self-image and weak masculine identity expose an individual to potential humiliation, whilst perverse fantasies and behaviour serve to raise his sense of self worth. Control within the perversion, as well as risk-taking are both important elements that raise self-esteem and, interestingly, Rosen emphasises the role of chance – particularly around puberty – in influencing the exact nature of the perverse solution.

Mervin Glasser, a psychoanalyst working at the Portman Clinic, was the first to describe the core complex in relation to perversions. His seminal paper (1988) focused on paedophilia, although his model is not restricted to child sexual abusers. His work is particularly helpful in his

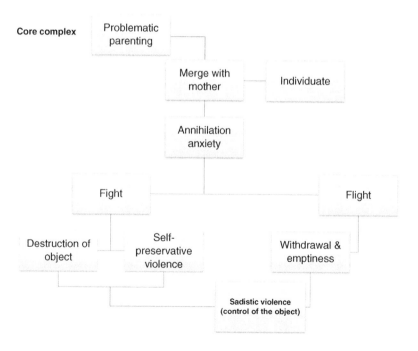

Figure 4.1 A schematic interpretation of the core complex

approach to defining aggression in sexual perversion: he refers to the differential function of sadistic and self-preservative aggression, an extremely helpful idea when trying to understand some sexual offences.

It is possible that Glasser, as a Freudian psychoanalyst, would be horrified to see the core complex outlined in schematic form as a flow chart! However, it has turned out to be a surprisingly simple and effective means of conveying complex ideas in a format that is easily digested.

It is important to remember that psychoanalysis is essentially a theory of normal, and universal, human development, and this includes the fundamental human dilemma at the root of the core complex: how to resolve the conundrum of achieving and maintaining a capacity for intimacy with and closeness to others without losing a sense of oneself as an independent individual with one's own 'mind.' The premise is that for the 'perverse' offender, this process has become problematic, leading to entrenched sexualised solutions. However, as we saw in Chapter 3 on the development of personality difficulties, the development of such sexualised scripts is complex and interdependent: the child brings his own propensities into the frame that interact with the relational environment and a perverse pathway develops. Therefore, a psychoanalytic understanding recognises that the child's experience in relation to caregivers may not represent observable reality as the child brings particular sensitivities to the parent-child dyad. Nevertheless in simplistic terms, the offender may have experienced or perceived being mothered as intrusive or smothering, and associated with a subtly hostile attitude to his developing masculinity. This experience needs to be coupled with experiences or perceptions of fathering that are either absent, cold or rejecting, thereby ensuring that there is only a weak or absent bond with a male father figure to 'rescue' the child from his maternal relationship; this ability to bond with an alternative parental figure is crucial for the development of a confident sense of self as a potent masculine individual, particularly as puberty hits.

As we saw in Chapter 3, the baby does not differentiate himself from his carer initially, and it is only over time that the child learns to separate and individuate from his primary carer (or what psychoanalysts call 'the love object'). Optimal development leads, eventually, to individuals being able to feel close to others, intimate with others, without losing a sense of themselves as an individual and separate person from the one they love. However, for the perverse individual, the experiences described in step one have led to difficulties with managing intimacy, which they have come to experience as 'annihilatory.' In this, Glasser is describing an overwhelming sense of anxiety in the individual, provoked by closeness to others, which habitually entails losing any sense of himself as a separate person.

The next step is one of responding to this overwhelming anxiety. Such threats – as we discussed in relation to attachment in Chapter 3 – are associated with fears for the survival of the self – and we are familiar with the fight/flight responses that can be triggered. In the perverse individual, flight is essentially a total withdrawal from connectedness to others, a safe situation but one associated with terrible feelings of emptiness and isolation. The second coping mode (fight) is to respond with aggression to the object of desire who engenders such conflicting feelings of longing, and fear of loss of self. Glasser acknowledges that this is essentially an adaptive self-preservative response to danger, built in by biology. However, the problem with attacking the 'love-object' is that the individual is destroying the very thing to which he longs to be close. This seemingly insoluble conflict is resolved in the perverse individual by the sexualisation of aggression. Glasser refers to this as sadistic aggression; by this he means that the perverse individual can engage with and relate to the love-object; by treating the love-object sadistically the aggression is expressed but does not destroy the other, and the individual retains control, holding the other at a 'safe distance.' We return to this idea of a 'safe distance' in the section below.

In the abstract it may well be that these ideas on the core complex are intellectually stimulating but have little clinical meaning or relevance for a non-analytic practitioner. Boxes 4.2 and 4.3 describe two cases – Terry and Barry – in which I have attempted to highlight those aspects of the history and presentation that are suggestive of various stages within the core complex. These case vignettes are hugely condensed; therefore the observations about indications of core complex mechanisms at play should be read as very tentative. I pick up on some additional observations below.

Box 4.2   Terry

Terry (aged 55) received a life sentence for the murder of a 38 year old woman. He was aged 30 at the time.

Terry described himself as the black sheep of the family: his mother had always wanted a girl *(annihilation anxiety)*, and used to buy him dolls for toys, and let his hair grow long. When he was six twin sisters were born and he felt that his mother then ignored him and sometimes belittled him. His father was a strict and critical man who seemed to be rather disappointed with his son *(problematic parenting)*.

(continued)

(continued)

Terry was then subject to terrible rages, when he would smash objects and become uncontrollable *(self-preservative aggression/fight)*. He recalled being sent to a child psychiatrist and had some vague memory of being in hospital after attacking another child; the rages stopped around the start of secondary school.

School was uneventful and Terry was described as quiet and quite bright although he had no friends *(withdrawal)*. Since leaving school he worked in the same computer firm for eight years until his index offence.

Terry has had no sexual relationships *(withdrawal/flight)*. However, around puberty he started to develop a vivid fantasy life *(sexualisation at puberty)* that became increasingly focused on raping women who he would imagine following down an isolated street late at night *(sadistic violence)*. Much of the detail of his fantasy was taken up with the act of following, anticipating the rape, and tying up the victim; he was less interested in the sexual element of the fantasy.

A series of rather minor events – having to move flat, a new manager at work, and a new female neighbour who tended to flirt with him, inducing a state of 'panic' in him *(annihilation anxiety)* – seemed to trigger the onset of the offence. Terry began to go out at night, actually following women. This progressed so that he was imagining raping them *(sadistic violence)*. Eventually he bought a knife and rope, and planned to carry out his fantasy. He followed a woman as she returned home late at night, and dragged her into an alleyway *(sadistic violence)*. When he began tying her up, she started to reason with him, quite calm and kind; this enraged him, and he screamed at her to shut up. However, when she persisted, he said he 'lost it totally' *(self preservative violence)* and 'came to' having strangled her.

The core complex was particularly helpful in enabling me to understand Terry's offence. I felt that the early trauma probably centred on his enmeshed relationship with his mother that was predicated on a shared deception that he was the girl she so longed for. One could say that Terry sacrificed his masculinity for his mother, and then felt betrayed and rejected. His father's coldness constrained Terry's ability to develop a masculine identity that might have helped him to survive this trauma. He had limited recall of his rages and we do not know whether he did in fact attack a child when he was young; however, the key fact is that he himself associates his development with a capacity for murderous rages, and there is a suggestion that it was the onset of puberty that led to him finding a sexualised solution for his anger. Interestingly, Terry was able to manage a stable perverse solution for many years; he balanced withdrawal in his external world with a sadistic fantasy life in his internal world. It was when this homeostasis was unbalanced – and I think it was the experience of the flirtatious neighbour at a time of disruption to his routine that was key – when external reality (the flirtatious neighbour) started to mesh with his internal fantasy life, and the conditions were set for him to carry out the offence. It was as though his perverse defences were breaking down and no longer 'working for him,' leading to escalation and an attempt to regain control. In my view, the primary motivation for the sexual attack was a sadistic one – to seek to control the love object, not destroy it – but for this to succeed, he needed the victim to behave exactly as he had fantasised she should behave, in terror. When in fact she was able to assume a semblance of reasonable control in response to his attack, a surge of anxiety resulted in the sexualisation breaking down so that what was revealed was the primitive aggression that underpinned it – the urge to destroy the other who evokes such conflicting feelings of longing and annihilation (as he experienced it in that incoherent moment). The core complex is particularly helpful in clarifying the function of the different types of violence within a single catastrophic offence.

Box 4.3   Barry

Barry (aged 25) was released from prison 18 months ago, having served 2 years of a 4 year determinate sentence for the indecent assault of a woman unknown to him. This offence had taken place after Barry had been continuously viewing pornography that fuelled his derogatory view of women; he went out and grabbed the breasts of a woman in the supermarket. He had two previous convictions for indecent exposure (at the ages of 17 and 19) which similarly involved stranger adult women in the street *(sadistic aggression?)*

Barry had completed the core SOTP in prison with a reasonable report. He subsequently worked with a female psychologist on

(continued)

(continued)

Healthy Sexual Relationships, and the discharge report highlighted concerns regarding sexual preoccupation and a diverse and complex range of deviant sexual fantasies *(sadistic aggression)*. Medication was recommended, as well as further individual work.

In the community, he was assessed and offered medication, which he refused as he 'didn't want to fill his body with toxic chemicals,' believing that a combination of renewed religious commitment and healthy living *(withdrawal)* would provide the means to avoid reoffending. Somewhat against his will, he was placed in the PD sex offender group-work programme, rather than being offered the individual work with a female therapist that he requested.

In the assessment, his manner had been rather odd, with veiled references to pornography, fantasies, and the 'need to confide . . . preferably in a woman with whom he would find it easier to talk openly' *(merging)*. In supervision, he was described as 'oily and secretive.' In the group, Barry sometimes engaged as an educator – the third group facilitator – but more often, he was sulky and withdrawn, apparently uninterested in the other group members *(withdrawal)*.

Background information on Barry was sparse. He was an only child with a close relationship with his mother who had strong religious beliefs that led to her criticising him at times when he showed evidence of 'wickedness.' On the other hand, he was her confidante. His father seemed to have been marginalised in the relationship and left a few years after he was born *(problematic parenting)*, resulting in the, absence of an effective male role model, possibly leaving him exposed to an overclose relationship with his mother. As an anxious child, Barry was subject to nightmares, and he often slept in his mother's bed as this comforted him *(merging)*. There was no evidence of actual sexual abuse. In adolescence and early adulthood, Barry's mother had a new boyfriend who stayed over occasionally. However, his nightmares continued and up until his prison sentence, he continued the habit of moving to her bed at night when troubled *(merging)*.

Towards the end of the group programme, Barry became depressed *(withdrawal)*. It later emerged that his mother had moved to Liverpool to be with her sister. His attempts to find work or to study had somehow come to nothing, and he was worried about the group ending. He was offered individual monthly support from one of the group therapists.

Barry represents a less terrifying type of sexual offender, but challenging and difficult to manage nevertheless. Drawing on the core complex to understand his offending was central to our decisions regarding treatment, and guided our management of his behaviour. With Barry, the clues to his perverse mechanisms were first apparent in his demeanour in interview; experience suggests that one should always be suspicious of individuals who want to discuss their sexual fantasies and masturbatory behaviour, coupled with requests to have individual work with female therapists. The experience of working with him felt similar to his rather evasive description of sharing a bed with his mother – too close, unboundaried but not quite sexually abusive – and we felt any concrete replication of this dynamic needed to be avoided in terms of therapy. Unfortunately, he rejected medication (see Chapter 5 for more explanation) and this reflects our wider experience with perverse offenders, who are often deeply ambivalent about therapy and terrified of losing their perverse solutions. It is true that he hated being in the group programme, sharing the facilitators with the other men, but we felt that this was important in restricting his access to any 'special relationship' and giving him an opportunity to develop his sense of masculine self. Over time, we discerned improvements in the way in which he learnt to relate to the others, and a significant reduction in behaviours suggesting sulky withdrawal. Interestingly it was his mother – as we understood it – who made the first move to sever their unhealthily close relationship, and his ensuing depression was the first opportunity for really meaningful engagement with him.

Fantasy as a regulator of self-esteem – practical applications

Psychoanalytic thinking around the meaning of repetitive sexually perverse functioning in individuals clearly highlights the dilemma that requires resolution: achieving rewarding intimacy by managing a longing for blissful closeness to others without laying oneself completely open to the potentially catastrophic (in psychological terms) consequences of such closeness to one's sense of self. The perverse sexual script provides the solution for some of our offenders, and the case vignettes above have tried to demonstrate the utility of these ideas in formulating complex cases, understanding the nature and function of the aggression, and making treatment decisions.

However, moving away from the psychoanalytic world for a moment, there is the question as to whether this way of thinking can help us with understanding the link between fantasy and behaviour and therefore with managing offenders in terms of risk. Perversion in psychoanalytic terms, and sexual self regulation in risk assessment terms are entirely compatible ideas; clearly persistent deviant sexual interests and habitual recourse to sexual fantasies to manage negative mood states or self esteem are both powerful high risk concerns that overlap to some considerable extent with ideas of perversion.

There are more problematic questions that arise though, most particularly the variable extent to which fantasy is linked to observable behaviour. We know, for example, that the general population is capable of engaging in highly unusual, violent or deviant fantasies – as perhaps evidenced by the Nancy Friday publications such as My Secret Garden (1973). We also know that there are individuals (a difficult to research group) who have a persistent sexual interest in children or in violent coercive rape, but who never step over the boundary into overt enactment of their wishes. Furthermore, over the past ten years or so, there have been thousands of prosecutions for the downloading of illegal sexual abuse images of children, associated with grave concerns regarding the potential risk of escalation to contact sexual offending. Yet, the follow up findings are fairly clear; such offenders (without prior sexual convictions) tend to present with a number of problematic characteristics in terms of self image, assertiveness and relational skills, as well as a capacity to be aroused by deviant images, and yet only 1–2% escalate over four years at risk to sexually assaulting a child (Seto, Hanson & Babchishin, 2011). There are also those paedophile offenders who state that recourse to pornography and fantasy has enabled them to avoid assaulting a child, although this has not been the subject of research studies. Finally, when working therapeutically with sexual offenders, practitioners will repeatedly have had the experience of many offenders denying that they had had deviant sexual fantasies prior to offending; of course, this may be a shame-avoiding technique, but the evidence suggests that we do need to take a flexible approach to the relationship between fantasy, self esteem and behaviour.

In a very practical way, we work with sexual offenders in the Challenge Project to think about fantasy in a much broader and less pathological way, 'using our imagination to create a story, or a day dream over which we have control' and moving away from constraining ourselves to purely sexual themes. We then link this to the idea of three functions (as shown in Table 4.1) described below:

Table 4.1 Understanding the function of imagination and fantasy

Fantasy name	Function for self-esteem	Non-offence related examples
Wish-fulfilment/ heroic longing	To boost self-esteem	Imagining winning the lottery; intervening to save a life, being able to fly
Vengeful fantasy	To restore self-esteem	Imagining 'getting one's own back', re-writing the script, coming out the winner – reversing the humiliation
Rehearsal fantasy	To practice an action in advance in order to improve performance	Imagining a job interview, imagining playing a part in a play and rehearsing the lines

1   **Imagining as a rehearsal**

Fantasy in this context is about anticipating an event and the way in which it may play out. A non-offending example might be preparing for a job interview, rehearsing interview scenes in one's mind and practicing answers to hypothetical questions. Clearly offence-relevant examples might include the building up to an offence with an increasing preoccupation with masturbating to rape fantasies, or to thoughts of touching the boy next door.

2   **Imagining as a means of boosting self esteem**

Fantasy in this context is about escaping into a world of wish-fulfilment, in which we create scenarios that make us feel better about ourselves. If we return to the idea of a job interview, a non-offending example would be to daydream about promotion, creating scenarios in which we are the boss; other common examples include daydreams about winning the lottery and giving away money, or acting heroically in dangerous situations. Offence-relevant examples tend to contain strong elements of romantic or seductive success associating the assaultative behaviour – disturbed as this may sound – with a themes of idealisation, longing and closeness associated with sexual fantasies in which the person is potent and desirable. However, it is also quite common to encounter non sexual fantasies that emphasise the offender's potential dangerousness – elaborate stories about mutilation, for example – and invite the awe or fear of others in response.

3   **Imagining as a means of restoring self esteem**

Fantasy in this context is about redressing the balance in response to a perceived humiliation or rejection by 'turning the tables.' Non-offending examples, in a job interview context, include revisiting a failed interview situation in one's mind but redesigning the scenario so that we gain the upper hand, or in some other way ensure that our interviewer is the one who is put down by our brilliant and cutting comments. Offence-relevant examples tend to include themes of vengeance that can be sexual – a violent rape scenario designed to achieve maximum humiliation of the victim – or more commonly aggressive, with the use of verbal or physical violence. In paedophilic fantasies, the other – the child – is small and vulnerable, and the individual, by implication, is in control.

Summary

In conclusion, whether one adopts a sophisticated psychoanalytic understanding to formulate why an offence might have happened, or reverts to a more pragmatic cognitive behavioural intervention, the central theme remains the same: perverse fantasies and behaviours provide a solution – albeit fleeting and ultimately unsatisfactory – to core intimacy dilemmas by regulating our self esteem, creating the illusion of control and thereby triumphing over trauma.

Note

1 The Portman Clinic is a London (UK) based National Health Service out-patient clinic, that provides specialist long-term psychoanalytically informed psychotherapeutic help to individuals who suffer from problems arising from sexual and violent behaviour.

References

Bateman, A. and Fonagy, P. (2006). *Mentalization-based Treatment for Borderline Personality Disorder: A Practical Guide*. Oxford: Oxford University Press.

Beck, A.T. (1975). *Cognitive Therapy and the Emotional Disorders*. Madison, CT: International Universities Press, Inc.

Boer, D. (ed.) (2016). *The Wiley Handbook on the Theories, Assessment, and Treatment of Sexual Offending. Volume II*. Chichester: John Wiley & Sons Ltd

Craissati, J., McClurg, G. and Browne, K. (2002). Characteristics of perpetrators of child sexual abuse who have been sexually victimised as children. *Sexual Abuse: A Journal of Research and Treatment, 14(3)*, 225–40.

Freud, A. (1993). *The Ego and the Mechanisms of Defence.* London: Karnac Books (original work published in 1936).

Freud, S. (1927). Fetishism (J. Strachey, trans.). In *The Complete Psychological Works of Sigmund Freud Vol. XXI* (pp. 147–57). London: Hogarth and the Institute of Psychoanalysis.

Friday, N. (1975). *My Secret Garden: Women's Sexual Fantasies.* UK: Virago Ltd.

Glasser, M. (1988). Psychodynamic aspects of paedophilia. *Psychoanalytic Psychotherapy, 3,* 121–35.

Miller, J. (1998). The enemy inside: An exploration of the defensive processes of introjecting and identifying with the aggressor. *Psychodynamic Counselling, 4,* 55–70.

Pfäfflin, F. (2016). Psychoanalytic treatment of sex offenders: A short historical sketch. In (ed.) D. Boer, *The Wiley Handbook on the Theories, Assessment, and Treatment of Sexual Offending. Volume II.* (pp. 1347–54). Chichester: John Wiley & Sons Ltd.

Rosen, I. (1979). Perversion as a regulator of self-esteem. In (ed.) I. Rosen, *Sexual Deviation (2nd Edition).* Oxford: Oxford University Press.

Seto, M.C., Hanson, R.K. and Babchishin, K. (2011). Contact sexual offending by men with online sexual offenses. *Sexual Abuse: A Journal of Research and Treatment, 23,* 124–45.

Stoller, R.J. (1975). *Perversion: The Erotic Form of Hatred.* New York: Pantheon.

Yakeley, J. (2010). *Working with Violence: A Contemporary Psychoanalytic Approach.* London: Palgrave Macmillan.

5 What might a good treatment intervention look like?

Introduction

There have been attempts to treat sexual offenders stemming back to the time of the Romans (see Marshall and Marshall, 2016, for an overview of this history); and developments in treatment models over the past 50 or so years have reflected the changes in psychological therapies during that time. Psychoanalysis was replaced by behaviourism and an emphasis on conditioning models, until the importance of cognitions began to be highlighted. Subsequent addiction models of sexually deviant behaviour eventually gave way to a more nuanced focus on individual developmental experiences and core beliefs (sometimes referred to as schemas).

The aim of this chapter is to focus on treatment interventions for high risk complex sexual offenders, building on the knowledge of the preceding chapters. An overview is presented of recent advances in our understanding of what interventions appear to have an impact on outcomes both for sexual offending and for personality disorder. However, the primary focus of the chapter is to provide the reader with ideas regarding the core issues that need to be considered in treatment, alongside some practical ideas as to how to address them. The chapter is heavily based on the experience of the Challenge Project, and therefore reflects our need to provide a resource-light intervention for a diverse group of high risk and complex sexual offenders residing in the community (many of whom may already have received treatment in prison). It is by no means the only way in which to deliver treatment for this group of individuals and other approaches could easily be justified. However, it is based on an integration of clinically applied research with 25 years of experience in delivering the programme.

Before reviewing the literature on treatment outcomes, it is worth pausing to consider what the definition of treatment, in this context, might be. Criminal justice agencies refer to 'interventions' rather than treatment or therapy, presumably because such 'programmes' tend to be delivered by practitioners without a wider formal therapy training. Nevertheless, such group interventions are explicitly cognitive behavioural in orientation, with some attention paid to therapeutic processes such as the establishment of a warm and non-confrontational rapport with the group members. In contrast, treatment provided by practitioners within forensic mental health services – including those delivered to offenders with a personality disorder – tend to refer to 'therapy' (sometimes also described as psycho-educational, supportive or intensive) and rely on practitioners with a core mental health training and additional therapy skills.

Chapter 6 focuses on the psychologically informed management of individuals with complex sexual offending histories; where this involves manipulating the environment or context within which the offender is held, or when in direct face-to-face contact with the offender, I refer to this as an **intervention**. That is, a broader term to describe a conscious and deliberate strategy, based on psychological principles, to help influence an individual's behaviour and his relationship with practitioners and agencies. **Treatment**, therefore – as defined here – is just one type of intervention; I use the term to refer to the delivery of an evidence-based package of direct intervention, in which the theoretical underpinning of the treatment is closely related to the content and process by which it is delivered. The aim of treatment is to alleviate the distress and/or the problem, in this instance, to reduce the likelihood of sexual recidivism. In other words, an intervention may be 'therapeutic' but it is not necessarily 'therapy.' This attempt to distinguish treatment from a wider toolkit of interventions can easily be criticised and may seem somewhat artificial. Furthermore, medical definitions of the treatment of a condition as compared to the management of a condition, clearly emphasise the intention of treatment to 'cure' rather than the latter's intention to 'control' disease. I return to this distinction later in the chapter.

Finally, it seems important to touch on the purpose of treating sexual offenders. Can treatment be for any legitimate purpose other than that of reducing sexual recidivism? In my view there are risks in allowing enthusiastic treating practitioners to emphasise psychological well-being or improved self-awareness as important outcomes of treatment; this often serves a defensive purpose, justifying outcome failures: an insightful or more contented recidivist is still a recidivist on our programme; and a sexual offender programme will endure or falter on the basis of its hard outcomes. For the purposes of this chapter, therefore, I will constrain myself to sexual recidivism as the primary outcome of concern.

The relevant evidence base for the treatment of sexual offenders

The 'what works' literature from criminal justice

Looking for and inevitably finding signs of positive change in the individuals whom we engage in therapy is understandable. It has therefore been a slow and painful process to shift our focus away from impressionistic observations onto outcomes that have greater empirical validity. The past 20 years or so has been characterised by tremendous efforts to establish the credibility of mainstream interventions for sexual offenders as significantly influencing outcomes in terms of recidivism. However, studies still remain flawed because of their methodological limitations within a sphere of work where there are many ethical constraints. Sample sizes are small, psychometric measures of change are hampered by socially desirable responding, comparison groups are difficult to match, and subjects are almost never randomly allocated to the treatment condition.

The debate – does treatment reduce the sexual recidivism rate of convicted sexual offenders? – remains as passionate as ever; knowledgeable views are diverse and the criticisms of recent well designed evaluations are vociferous. Two fairly recent meta-analytic reviews concluded with some cautious optimism: Loesel and Schmucker (2005) examined 69 studies comprising more than 20,000 sexual offenders, and found that those receiving treatment sexually recidivated 6% less than the untreated controls: that is, 11% versus 17% sexual recidivism, equating to a reduction of over a third in the rate of reoffending. Hanson, Bourgon, Helmus and Hodgson (2009) reviewed 22 reasonable quality studies and found an 8% difference between the sexual recidivism rate of treated versus untreated sexual offenders (11% and 19% respectively); this equated to a reduction of over 40% in the rate of reoffending.

These meta-analyses, as well as a wider body of evaluation of criminal justice interventions, found that well-articulated cognitive-behavioural therapy (CBT) models demonstrated the best results, although this perhaps relates more to the number and rigour of CBT studies than to clearly establishing that other therapy models do not work. Most importantly, the analyses reliably show that the treatment effect is greatest in those who pose a higher risk; indeed, those who are deemed to be low risk on assessment tools are repeatedly shown to recidivate at slightly higher levels following treatment than those low risk offenders who do not receive treatment (Hanson *et al.*, 2009). Olver (2016 p. 1315) provides some further examples of the iatrogenic effect of programmes essentially 'over-treating' low risk sexual offenders and generating very poor outcomes in terms of sexual recidivism.

Despite the encouraging findings from the meta-analytic reviews, it is worth mentioning two robust evaluations that have yielded disappointing results. Marques, Weideranders, Day *et al.* (2005) applied the relapse prevention model (based on ideas of addiction) to sexual offenders incarcerated in California, USA; they were impressive in their attempts to design a methodologically robust study, with the use of random allocation of volunteer offenders to treatment and control groups, as well as comparison with non-volunteer offenders (that is, those who met the criteria but did not want treatment). There was a follow up period of five years at risk in the community. The results were clear: there was no treatment effect in terms of significant differences in sexual or violent offending; this was true for type of offence/victim, risk level and time to re-offence. Furthermore, although scores on a number of pre-post treatment psychometric measures improved as a result of treatment, none of these changes were significantly associated with subsequent sexual recidivism.

The most recent evaluation of note is Mews, di Bella and Purver's (2017) analysis of the England and Wales prison-based sex offender treatment programme (SOTP). Prison programmes in England and Wales go through a robust accreditation process and are then rolled out extensively across the prison estate, with tightly managed procedures for ensuring treatment integrity and the supervision of prison staff who deliver the programme. The evaluation comprised 2,562 sexual offenders in prison who started the treatment between 2000 and 2012, matched to 13,219 comparison sexual offenders on the basis of 87 matching factors. The follow-up period averaged eight years at risk in the community and the overall recidivism rate was 38% with a sexual recidivism rate of 7.5%. In essence, it was found that 10% of treated sexual offenders sexually recidivated compared to 8% of the matched comparison offenders; furthermore, 4.4% of treated sexual offenders committed at least one child abuse image reoffence compared to 2.9% of the matched comparison offenders. Of particular relevance to this book, in terms of complexity, 16.9% of those sexual offenders who were categorised as high or very high risk on the Risk Matrix 2000 (comprising around 25% of the treated sample) sexually recidivated as compared to 13.7% of the matched comparison offenders.

In terms of the Challenge Project programme evaluation, an overview of results was presented in Chapter 1. However, it is worth reiterating here the outcomes of the more recent evaluation of high risk sexual offenders in the community group programme, although the methodology used was by no means robust. The early evaluations (for example, Craissati, South, & Bierer, 2009) clearly found that the programme was ineffective with low and medium risk sexual offenders, but demonstrated a significant treatment effect with higher risk sexual offenders and/or with those who reported significant levels of childhood adversity and more pervasive psychological disturbance. As the programme increasingly targeted this high risk group of sexual offenders with personality difficulties (Craissati & Blundell, 2013), we found that our sexual recidivism rate for those in treatment – based on an average of four years at risk – was 11% (dropping to 9% if the non-completers were excluded) and 3% recidivated violently. This compares favourably with the prison SOTP outcomes for high risk sexual offenders cited above, but we did not have access to a local meaningful comparison group. Our most recent evaluation (Hopton, van Gerko & Craissati, 2018) has been in response to taking on a greater number of offenders who have previously refused treatments and who have antisocial and violent backgrounds: we have been able to identify that two Stable 2007 items (impulsivity and lack of cooperation with supervision – see Chapter 2 for more information on Stable 2007) as well as alcohol use and an external locus of control, are significantly associated with a return to prison for non-compliance. Two different Stable 2007 items – emotional identification with children and deviant sexual interests – are significantly associated with our sexual recidivists (mostly comprising child sexual abuse image offences rather than contact sexual offences). Whilst these findings are unsurprising, they do help us to review our treatment programme, and make changes to try and tackle these difficulties as they arise.

The 'effective therapy' literature for working with personality disorder, from a mental health perspective

The focus for therapies in the mental health system has been on emotionally unstable personality disorder, with some additional but limited work with antisocial personality disorder. Interventions for other types of personality disorder have rarely been evaluated robustly, and indeed, the Cochrane Review Groups have withdrawn their protocols for interventions for both narcissistic and avoidant personality disorders due to difficulties in identifying potentially suitable studies.

Emotionally unstable personality disorder has been the target of a number of commonly compared therapies: Dialectical Behaviour Therapy (DBT), Mentalisation Based Therapy (MBT), Transference-focused Therapy (TFP), and Schema Focused Therapy (SFT). DBT, MBT and SFT all contain elements of psycho-education as well as more exploratory techniques; they tend to offer a combination of individual and group work; they attend to attachment processes within the therapeutic relationship whilst remaining careful not to trigger overwhelming attachment anxieties; they offer telephone containment for difficult periods outside the scheduled therapy contacts; and the therapist is fairly active and directive within the sessions. All four therapies are equally able to demonstrate significantly greater effectiveness than standard care or non-expert therapies, but the evidence to support the superiority of one of the therapies over another is not robust. DBT – the most widely studied of the therapies – has also established that the skills training component is the most important element in order to effect sustained therapeutic change; that is, DBT is most effective at reducing the frequency of behavioural problems associated with impulsivity, but is less effective at improving mood states or interpersonal functioning.

So, the evidence hints at the possibility that there are common characteristics to the four treatment models that contain clues as to the source of their effectiveness. Bateman and Tyrer (2002) have described these common characteristics as described above, delivered within a clear philosophy and model of care that is understood by the therapists (or the team) and the clients/offenders alike.

Therapeutic progress with antisocial personality disorder alone (ASPD) has been much less encouraging and less widely studied; meta-analytic approaches have not been able to identify robust and sustained outcomes in terms of recidivism, aggression or social functioning. In fact the most promising results have come from studies looking at ASPD and substance misuse, where reduction in substance misuse was measured following contingency management (where progress in not using substances is rewarded) and cognitive behavioural interventions. These findings are mirrored in the emerging evidence for the significant treatment effect achieved when working with couples where domestic violence and substance misuse are both present (for example, O'Farrell, Fals-Stewart, Murphy *et al.*, 2004): although these studies do not take a diagnostic approach to personality, we know from the literature that pervasive psychological difficulties will often be found in perpetrators of domestic violence.

The one published randomised control trial in the community, for people with ASPD, found that a cognitive behavioural intervention was a relatively expensive option compared to treatment as usual, with no significant effect on reducing anger or aggression (Davidson, Halford, Kirkwood *et al.*, 2010). These findings, perhaps, exemplify the challenge in demonstrating a functional link between personality type and the offending behaviour as interventions have been demonstrably more successful with the latter than the former.

There are a few examples of studies with a wider group of personality disordered individuals: a large multi-centred randomised control trial of schema therapy in the Netherlands included a full range of personality types (Bernstein, D., Nijman, H., Karos, K., *et al.*, 2012). This study established the superiority of SFT as compared to treatment as usual or clarification-oriented psychotherapy, as well as the superiority of exercise-based schema therapy training to lecture-based training.

A note: anticipating problems with treatment drop out

Treatment refusal, as we established in Chapter 2, is not associated with elevated risk of sexual recidivism and, for example, in the Marques *et al.* (2005) and the Craissati *et al.* (2009) studies cited above, those who were not placed in treatment had better outcomes in terms of recidivism that those who commenced treatment but dropped out. Treatment drop out is, however, of particular salience in relation to offenders with persistent and pervasive psychological difficulties (PPPD). Not only are the variables associated with increased likelihood of drop out strongly linked to personality disorder traits (McMurran & Theodosi, 2007), but those who drop out are generally about twice as likely to recidivate sexually or violently, compared to a matched control group (Craissati *et al.*, 2009; Marques *et al.*, 2005). There is, therefore, **a strongly interconnected relationship between risk, PPPD and dropping out of treatment: they are all underpinned by traits such as impulsivity, impoverished problem solving and emotional volatility, as well as behaviours such as thrill seeking and substance misuse**.

Summary

In answer to the question 'what does the relevant evidence base for the treatment of sexual offenders tell us?' we could probably conclude the following:

- There is no evidence to justify the treatment of low risk offenders.
- The preferred model of treatment for medium risk sexual offenders, including those without complex PPPD, is cognitive behavioural in orientation.
- For those who are higher risk with more PPPD, it is important to anticipate problems with treatment non-completion and the concerns that drop out raises for a significantly higher rate of sexual recidivism.

- Treatment for complex sexual offenders needs to comprise individual as well as group modes of delivery, and a mix of psycho-education, skills development, and more exploratory elements.
- It is important that the philosophy and model of care is very explicitly explained and understood.

Whether the above list is sufficient to protect treatment from the possibility of failure is unclear. The criminal justice response in England and Wales to the disappointing outcome of the prison programme (Mews *et al.*, 2017) has been to roll out new programmes that avoid any discussion of the offence and the chain of events leading up to it, in order to focus on skills development in the key dynamic risk areas. The implication is that the previous programmes focused excessively on offence-specific features such as developing victim empathy, and comprehensive offence accounts for which offenders were encouraged to take full responsibility. This shift in focus undoubtedly represents an efficient means of providing valuable interventions for a wide range of offenders – including those in denial – but might perhaps be criticised for having dropped the idea of 'narrative' from offence-relevant work (see below for further discussion).

An alternative interpretation of the uncertain impact of treatment on sexual recidivism is to examine whether the fundamental model of treatment as a curative dose of 'medicine' to alleviate a condition, is the wrong model. Take, for example, the difference in approach to treating tonsillitis and diabetes (as seen from the lay person's perspective). Tonsillitis, for the most part, does not require any specialist intervention, but when it is particularly virulent, it may be appropriate to prescribe a dose of antibiotics that should be taken over a time limited period. Diabetes, on the other hand, requires a much more varied and flexibly delivered approach: depending on type and severity, it may be necessary to inject insulin on a daily basis, although for others, diet and exercise may be sufficient; self help groups may be the most effective maintenance intervention for some, although others will have a wildly fluctuating course of illness that ultimately requires surgery in relation to complications. The analogy with sexual offending is clear: for the majority of lower risk sexual offenders, there is a limited requirement for treatment. For those higher risk offenders, with PPPD, intervention models that rely on a particular intervention dosage (a longer more intensive treatment programme) are probably flawed, and a more flexible management approach is required longer term. This idea of flexibility and 'light touch' interventions for the more disturbed does appear to fly in the face of traditional Risk-Need-Responsivity principles; that is, I suggest that responsivity factors dictate that 'dosage' approaches to the risk and need elements of this subgroup of sexual offenders should be adjusted in a counter-intuitive fashion.

Acknowledging our theoretical influences

There is no shame in acknowledging that almost all the best ideas are derivative! Our programme has been heavily influenced over the years by researchers and academic theorists as well as by skilled practitioners. The more we have focused on working with complexity, the more we have needed to develop what could be termed a 'therapeutic toolkit,' drawing on the best and most useful of what we can find. There are risks in adopting this eclectic approach, most important of which is losing a sense of a core philosophy and model of care that has coherence and meaning. When a therapy loses its stable centre, it is cast adrift, and potentially incoherent and ineffective. Therefore, although the following provide a brief overview of our influences, we conclude this section with a clear articulation of the model of care for the Challenge Project programme.

Understanding and working with defences

Chapter 4 clearly demonstrated the influence of psycho-analytic ideas in improving our ability to formulate an understanding of sexual offending. However, in terms of enabling facilitators to engage with group members in understanding the ways in which they protect themselves from negative feelings, we have drawn heavily from Malan's (1979) enormously accessible book on individual psychotherapy: this is a 'how to' approach to the interpretation of defences, with immensely helpful case vignettes – none of them forensic in nature – and careful explanations regarding the timing and intensity of observations. The triangles in this book are an adaptation of Malan's triangles – the 'triangle of conflict' and the 'triangle of person' (p. 80) – and the facilitators have learnt to modify their work with offenders to fit with their capacity to tolerate piercing observations that have the potential to cause intense anxiety.

Understanding 'life traps' (schemas), schema modes and coping styles

Schemas refer to core beliefs that are developmentally determined and enduring, underpinning many of the cognitive distortions that are more apparent in an individual's conscious mind. There has been a good deal of work on sexual offender-specific schemas – for example, Ward and Keenan (1999) – with reference to implicit theories that sexual offenders hold about the world. However, in terms of working with sexual offenders with PPPD, we have preferred to develop a psycho-educational approach with the offenders in which they learn to identify their life traps (schemas) in line with mainstream SFT. There is a helpful website – www.schematherapy.com – that provides guidance, and signposts where the materials can be purchased.

With simplified materials, group members find the work on schemas and on coping styles – surrender, avoid, overcompensate – immensely helpful. We use schema modes to help with those elements of the 'here and now' experiences that 'press my buttons' (see section below). For sexual offenders who may find abstract concepts challenging, and who struggle to piece together their life experiences in a meaningful way, schema related ideas are sufficiently concrete to enable them to develop their restricted emotional vocabulary and bring order to what they experience as bewildering.

The five principles of motivational interviewing (MI)

Regardless of experience and knowledge, facilitators are sometimes pushed to their limits by the hostile, defensive or minimising statements made by group members; these tend to go in waves, not always predictably, and can catch the best of facilitators off guard. Navigating these choppy waters can be challenging, and a reminder of the five principles of MI is always helpful. These are summarised in Dowsett and Craissati (2007, pp. 111–16), and laid out in detail in Mann (1996) in relation to working with sexual offenders. To recap briefly here, notably in relation to the challenges posed by particularly hostile individuals with PPPD:

1   *Express empathy* with warmth and honesty, validating the group member's experience in a manner that they can tolerate. For example, be warmly matter-of-fact in acknowledging how angry an individual might be at having to attend a group programme that they feel is a waste of time (avoiding an overly emotional tone).
2   *Avoid argumentativeness*, particularly in relation to provocative statements about an element of the offence, or commonly with more antisocial group members, avoid trying to persuade them that they were subjected to abuse as a child ('weak' in their eyes).
3   *Roll with resistance* but continue to be curious and avoid imposing your view of the world. It is often helpful to highlight different perspectives – the group member's view as contrasted with the facilitator's tentative thoughts, or to 'think aloud' about what is happening ('I can see that I'm trying to push you too much in a direction you don't think is relevant').

4   *Deploy discrepancy* as a most useful tactic when group members are making strenuous efforts to avoid any indication of psychological vulnerability or shameful admissions that they experience as humiliating. Emphasise the difference between how they see themselves and how others see them, or the difference between them as they were five years ago, with no idea that they would be labelled a sexual offender, and as they are now.

5   *Support self-efficacy* in ways that the group members feel is meaningful. There is no point talking about strengths in the context of a controlling risk-avoidant plan that has no realistic prospect of changing. However, teaching the group members to assess their own risk using shared tools is a good example of supporting self-efficacy; be honest about the sexual recidivism rates, and show the group member how he can ensure he is in the 'non-offending' portion of his risk group.

Thinking under pressure (mentalisation)

Although we use SFT as an important component of the group content, we draw on Mentalisation Based Therapy (MBT) for developing the facilitators' skills when addressing group processes. MBT, as a model, is rooted in attachment theory (see Chapter 3 for more information) and postulates that failing to mentalise leads to marked difficulties in maintaining self-identity, affect regulation and impulsivity. Mentalising is the process of holding your own mind in mind, whilst also attending to what may be going on in the minds of others; improving one's capacity to mentalise is therefore hypothesised to enhance an individual's ability to manage complex interpersonal and social situations and relationships (Bateman & Fonagy, 2006).

MBT takes a curious, non-expert stance, that is active and questioning – all of which sits well with group members with PPPD. It encourages facilitators to own those aspects of their behaviour that may have triggered habitual and dysfunctional responses in the group members, rather than emphasise the group member's failure. For example, in talking to an offender in the group who was caught shoplifting during the Christmas break, facilitators own their failure to organise enough support for the group member, rather than speculating about his 'hostile' behaviour. However, the most helpful aspect of MBT is its emphasis on three common types of failure of mentalisation and their modes:

Pretend mode tends to be associated with inner feelings of emptiness, and is often manifest as a form of intellectualising or pseudo-mentalising. There may be endless inconsequential talk; thoughts and feelings may be contradictory and often changing; description of their inner world seems to bear no resemblance to external reality. With sexual offenders, this may also be apparent in an ability to say all the right things in therapy, with apparently genuine conviction, but then, almost simultaneously, to go out and do 'the wrong thing.' Challenging such empty talk can provoke a strong and unhelpful reaction because of the feelings of emptiness that it is masking; it can also induce a sort of frozen and helpless 'glazed' response in the facilitators who experience any attempt at exploration or connection as ineffective.

Psychic equivalence refers to the excessively concrete interpretation of a person's mental reality as manifestly real and the same as outer reality. Frightening thoughts about the intentions of others are experienced as real and terrifying, and no other interpretations are possible. This adds both drama and risk in terms of the exaggerated reaction of group members in their everyday encounters with others, and the seriousness with which they suddenly experience their own and others' thoughts and feelings. Sexual offenders may perceive devastating rejection or humiliation perpetrated towards them by others, and reject all alternative possibilities. The group facilitators may experience the group member as rigid and hostile in his claims that he knows what the facilitators are thinking, and it is easy to fall into the trap of becoming defensive in response.

Teleological mode refers to changes in mental states that are assumed to be real only when confirmed by physically observable action contingent upon the individual's feeling or wish. In other words, it is not enough to offer commitment and reliability as evidence of facilitator concern, as these will be experienced by the individual with PPPD as self evidently taken for granted. It is only when a facilitator deviates from the routine in a way that is contingent with the offender's wishes that there can be a sense of meaningful control from the group member's point of view. Sexual offenders who engage with a particular facilitator in sexually explicit banter or flirtation may be seeking to elicit a 'special' response that confirms the intimacy of the relationship; for others, they may seek to dupe the facilitators with excessive travel claims, or take up disproportionate time in the group following a self harm attempt.

The helpful aspect of MBT and the modes of mentalising is that it enables facilitators to move away from ideas of the offender as 'manipulative' and 'attention-seeking,' in order to understand that complex sexual offenders repeatedly engage in problematic ways of thinking about their own mind and the minds of others. Facilitators are encouraged to explore the antecedents to a mentalisation failure, and also to own their own mentalising processes – that is, to clearly state what he/she is thinking and how he/she arrived at a conclusion about what the group member is thinking or feeling.

What might a 'good life' look like?

The Good Lives Model (GLM) for sexual offenders has garnered considerable support over the past ten years or so (Fortune & Ward, 2013), although it is not without its critics, particularly those who emphasise the importance of the risk, needs, responsivity (RNR) model that has dominated the criminal justice world for some time. There is a useful website of resources – www.goodlivesmodel.com – and an example of the debate can be found in Criminal Justice and Behavior (Andrews, Bonta, & Wormith, 2011; Ward, Yates & Willis, 2012). It is important to remember that there is almost no published evidence to support GLM as an effective model for reducing sexual recidivism; however, what GLM lacks in evidence base it makes up for in terms of appeal. In essence, it has been enthusiastically adopted by practitioners, and welcomed by sexual offenders, for its focus on positive approach (rather than avoidance) goals, and a strengths-based stance for treatment. The model fits particularly well with desistance theory, a model for understanding offending and risk that we will return to in Chapter 6 (Laws & Ward, 2011).

In brief, Ward and colleagues have drawn widely from psychological and sociological research to identify between nine and eleven primary goods – shared human values that relate to states of mind, characteristics and experiences linked to human dignity and universal human rights. It is postulated that all humans seek out these primary goods to some degree but individuals give weight to specific goods that reflect their personal priorities. Sexual offending can represent a direct attempt to satisfy a primary good (for example, when a child sexual abuser seeks intimacy with a victim), or an indirect attempt, when in an attempt to satisfy a primary good, something goes wrong (for example, when an incest offender's adult relationship falters, and he turns instead to his daughter for solace and a restoration of his self esteem). Using the GLM for treatment involves taking into account each sexual offender's priorities, and the problems they encounter in achieving their goals. These might include difficulties with capacity, scope, means or coherence.

A working model of care (the Challenge Project)

Before moving on to describe some of the practicalities of delivering treatment, it is important to pause, in order to try and articulate a suggested philosophy and model of care that is shared between facilitators and group members on the Challenge Project. Adopting an integrative approach requires this articulation if it is not to disintegrate into 'a bit of a muddle,' with an associated loss of control and focus within the progress.

Our group work programme's model of care is articulated as follows:

> Sexual offending is a relational offence, by which we mean that both the assault itself and the victim – whatever he or she might represent – has meaning for the offender in the context of his own life history and attachment difficulties. We deliver a structured, evidence based, and offence-relevant content to the programme that provides the framework that enables us to explore the relational processes that emerge within the practitioner-offender-group triad. These emerging dynamics are included in our scope, as offering the opportunity for potentially reparative experiences that may be symbolic of earlier attachment systems. With the integration of psycho-educational content with relational perspectives, we aim to improve skills in the articulation of more sophisticated emotional states, and to develop the capacity to think at times when emotional states have previously tended to cloud thinking. The goal is to introduce personally relevant and meaningful ideas of agency, self control and choice in relation to offending and wider relating: to find meaning in the past, to manage the present, and to plan for a meaningful offence-free future.

We also have a service user-friendly version of this model of care, which is shared with all group members and returned to at regular intervals during the programme.

Delivering a group treatment programme

For the rest of this chapter, we focus on the delivery of the programme. There are a number of helpful books available for mainstream sexual offender treatment delivery (for example, Marshall & Marshall, 2009; Stinson & Becker, 2018). Here, we are focusing simply on the necessary additional considerations when engaging complex high risk – and often highly ambivalent – sexual offenders in a community programme, most of whom are attending following their release from a fairly lengthy prison sentence. We conclude with a list of the most frequently asked questions.

Process considerations

These fall into three phases: before the group starts, for the duration of the group programme, and following completion of the group.

1   **Before the group starts**

There are a few key steps to take before an individual offender joins the group and we try to complete them within one to two sessions. For individuals who are prone to failing in the community, delays tend to expose the agencies to unnecessary risks.

An individual provisional *case formulation* needs to be written, that integrates an understanding of the offence, with a risk assessment and the results of any psychometrics. This takes the form of a brief letter written to the offender himself and copied to his referrer. The key is to anticipate possible issues that may emerge in the hothouse atmosphere of the group and to remain alert to the dominant risk concerns. Over the years, we have reduced our use of psychometrics to the bare minimum, largely on account of them annoying the group members and providing very little assistance with identifying treatment needs or predicting outcomes. We have been using a self-report personality measure, given the focus of our programme, but we are considering dropping that too, as antisocial group members are reporting average healthy profiles that reflect how they see themselves and how they wish to be seen by us but bear little resemblance to their life stories. Our last remaining pre-post measure, that continues to provide us with useful information, is the Locus of Control questionnaire (LoC). The LoC identifies that many of our group members commence treatment with external traits – believing events in the world to be outside their control – and they shift over the course of treatment to believing to a greater extent that they have control over events (McAnena, Craissati & Southgate, 2016). The LoC therefore fits with our emphasis on agency as a key ingredient of change.

There is often a need to *persuade* the sexual offender as to why he should participate in the group. We have touched on motivational interviewing in the sections above, and in Chapter 6, we talk a little more about psychologically informed management. The key issue for joining the group is an open discussion with the individual offender regarding his areas of vulnerability and risk, and an honest view of the advantages and disadvantages of the group programme. This is not the same as suggesting it is optional, something that we only do if an individual is self-referring to the group. We make no assumption that a group member will enjoy the group, or find it helpful to talk about his private states of mind with others; we take an enlightened self-interest approach – why it might be worth something to the offender if he gets through the programme and receives a reasonably positive post-treatment report. We warn offenders very clearly about the change in sexual recidivism rates linked to dropping out of treatment prematurely.

The **rules of engagement** include expectations of attendance and the limits of confidentiality. For habitual rule-breakers, it is important to reduce the opportunities to fail; we have two explicit rules – turn up (with a 15 minute lee-way for lateness) and contribute (carefully undefined so that we have some flexibility!) – and one implicit rule that we state openly if we think it might be a possibility – no physical fighting with other group members. Missed sessions are rated as 'acceptable' (for example, sickness), or 'unacceptable' (for example, feeling low), but we are careful not to box ourselves into a corner with rigid rules about the number of sessions that are deemed allowable. Confidentiality is only a problem if the risk assessment has been inadequate, and surprises crop up in the programme. The preliminary formulation and risk letter is shared; brief reports on each module are completed, as well as the discharge report, and these are also formal and shared, with an opportunity for the offender to have his comments recorded. We deal with new risk information, broadly speaking, by determining whether it is historical and in keeping with the known risk assessment (confidential), historical but significantly changing the risk assessment (not confidential), impending but vague (confidential) or impending and specific (not confidential). Our primary aim is to prevent further offences taking place but our preference is for the offender himself to know where the boundaries of confidentiality lie, and to retain control of decisions to breach those boundaries. Group members have invariably been affected by experiences of authority figures in their childhood behaving in an unreliable, duplicitous, or apparently hypocritical manner; we anticipate that there will be dynamic processes in the group that have the potential to replicate these experiences, pushing facilitators into unwanted roles of 'betrayer.'

Finally, a quick note about medication. This is often felt to be a last resort for sexual offenders but our experience is that medication plays a significant role with our complex group of offenders. For those with repetitive sexual offending or those with marked histories of sexual preoccupation (not necessarily including deviant sexual interests), medication may well comprise the most important first step in rehabilitation. Unfortunately we often struggle to persuade potential group members to consider medication as they put forward spurious reasons as to why it is not necessary; with the benefit of hindsight, we now see these excuses as symptomatic of the anxiety experienced at the thought of losing the intensity of their habitual sexual coping mechanisms. The medication options fall into the two categories of anti-depressants and anti-libidinals and more detailed information can be found for the UK at http://www.forensicnetwork.scot.nhs.uk/documents/medication%20for%20sex%20offenders%20protocol.pdf.; see also Thibaut, de la Barra, Gordon *et al.*, (2010) for international guidance on the biological treatment of paraphilias. Although a systematic review (Khan, Ferriter, Huband *et al.*, 2015) found limited evidence and were critical of the methodology of the studies, results for sexual offenders with poor sexual self regulation seem promising.

2   **For the duration of the group programme**

Often, the greatest gains are made when there are difficulties within the group process; and the facilitators need to be supported to work with these ruptures that they often experience as exhausting challenges to their competence. They need to be encouraged to embrace some turbulence within the group as helpful material rather than seek out obedient and diligent group members who are not emotionally engaged in the task. Such **therapeutic processes** are described in much greater detail in Craissati (2016) but it is worth mentioning here the Therapeutic Cycle Model (TCM; Pfafflin, Bohmer, Cornehl, & Mergenthaler, 2005) which provides a very helpful overarching framework for thinking about such processes. TCM measures two concepts – emotional and cognitive regulation operationalised as the amount of emotion and abstraction found in psychotherapy transcripts. Four patterns are described:

- *Relaxing*, which is characterised by low emotion and low abstraction where the client is undisturbed by what is happening
- *Reflection*, which is characterised by high abstraction with the patient being uninvolved emotionally
- *Experiencing* where there is high emotional involvement but little or no reflection
- *Connecting* where there is high emotional involvement and abstraction, so that the patient expresses their feelings while displaying an understanding of the issues.

Clearly there is a place for each of these four patterns, but our aim is to try and achieve connection as the optimum condition for change to occur.

Over the course of the first ten weeks or so of the group, some offenders exhibit extremely irritating interpersonal behaviours; we find that with some attention to the problem, the **settling in period** is over by month three. These problems can often be anticipated: for example, those offenders from large neglectful families are often 'attention-seeking' in relation to the therapists, excluding other group members; those from highly inter-dependent and enmeshed relationships with a sole parent tend to sulk in response to their new 'siblings' in the group. For others with schizoid traits, they may lack more complex social skills, whilst more antisocial others may experience the group as unbearably humiliating at first and respond aggressively. These dynamics are understood in the formulation, but often managed at first in the group with a behavioural approach – ignoring undesirable behaviours and positively reinforcing desirable interactions – with surprisingly positive results. We are explicit about the difficulties, when this can be tolerated by the individual concerned, and enlist other group members in a sensitive manner to support the offender.

Each group member has one of the facilitators allocated as his **individual therapist**, and we offer fortnightly or monthly sessions to complement the group programme. These can be used as required, but are always important as a link to the offender's life outside the group. The individual facilitator is responsible for implementing the treatment plan, in terms of liaising with the psychiatrist if medication needs to be considered, or accessing additional support or a work project. Outside the formal reporting parameters, we keep in touch with the referring professional in terms of acknowledging sessions attended or missed, and noting any emerging significant concerns regarding mental health, risk or social circumstances that might require extra support.

We pay considerable attention to the way in which we structure tasks within the group, in line with the **mentalising modes** described above. The propensity for the group to engage in pretend mode – pseudo-mentalising – is overwhelming when asked to contribute to a general group discussion, and each group member habitually takes on his assigned role in that discussion – the silent one, the avoidant one, the anxiously compliant one and the dramatic one. Breaking up the group into a variety of sub-groupings shakes up these dynamics: we often work in two halves, each with a facilitator, or put members into pairs that are similar or sometimes diverse. We often ask one group member to find out information from another, and to report back on behalf of his partner, a task that many find enormously difficult. The group members make assumptions about sameness and difference in the group, and we expose these assumptions whenever we have the opportunity. We put considerable emphasis on role play, ensuring that the facilitators expose their inadequacy as actors first, before expecting the group members to follow suit!

In a similar vein, we pay considerable attention to '*holding the group member in mind*' when he is not in the group. In line with teleological thinking, we know that offenders with PPPD struggle to trust that those in positions of control and authority are what they purport to be; they find it difficult to accept a collaborative non-judgemental professional relationship for what it is. We therefore make considerable effort to ring group members within five minutes of them not attending within the deadline; we text them the day of the group to remind them; we pay their travel expenses; we write them sick notes if they happen to be in work (rarely the case); and we support their housing applications where this is possible and appropriate. If there is a crisis, or if we are concerned about them, we are visibly and actively supportive. Furthermore, if a group member is recalled to prison, for whatever, reason, we keep their chair in the group until we know the outcome of their recall and we visit them in prison. The group are told about what has happened and are asked to write a letter to them – as well as a letter from the facilitators – to acknowledge what has happened in a supportive fashion. Interestingly, this is a particularly difficult task for the group members who find it very difficult to show compassion – it is as though they must distance themselves from the 'failed' group member, in order to deny their own anxiety about failing. We never close the case – remaining in letter contact and inviting the group member back to the group – unless the individual asks to be left alone.

3   **Following completion of the group**

Although some group members clearly cannot wait to finish the group programme, it is important not to underestimate the extent to which many of them have become attached – despite themselves – to the group, the facilitators, and/or the routine of attending. In all cases, it is important to plan for the *loss of the structure* and contact that is associated with completing a programme. Even more importantly, many high risk sexual offenders with PPPD, paradoxically, will pose a higher risk of sexual recidivism during the ensuing few months if they feel neglected as a result of having done well in the group and they will feel angry at the reduction in supervision associated with this treatment success. As one offender said to me about a prison group facilitator:

> *She could not have been more helpful to me whilst I was in the group, but when I put in an application to see her after the group had finished, she didn't even reply, I was just a tick in a box for her.*

For the offender, the significance of this experience went far beyond the understandable irritation that any of us might experience when an over-stretched practitioner is unresponsive.

For the majority of group members, they continue with their individual therapy, often delivered as a supportive 'dose' every one to two months. Our two day relapse prevention group has turned into more of a **maintenance** group and those ex-group members who tend to be more dependent and emotionally vulnerable attend on an annual basis, finding that '*the top up stops me becoming complacent.*' Increasingly we have developed peer support mechanisms – a weekly café, mentors, and a social enterprise – that offer on-going support under the supervision of staff (Jeffcote, van Gerko, & Nicklin, 2018).

Programme content

The content of our programme is, at first glance, fairly indistinguishable from that of most mainstream sexual offender treatment programmes, although it would be true to say that we put far less emphasis on group members arriving at the 'correct' understanding of their behaviour, and we do not in any way focus on those cognitive distortions that result in minimising of offending behaviour. With our emphasis on the learning from therapies for non-offenders with personality difficulties, we probably place more emphasis on problematic interpersonal dynamics, and the role of sex in regulating self esteem, and we are more likely to consider the group content as one very small part of an overarching intervention that includes, but is not restricted to, a group programme.

Our approach to the programme content can be divided into a focus on three areas overall: the past, the present and the future.

The past: the redemptive narrative

We adhere to Maruna's assertion (2001) that one element of desistance in high risk repeat offenders is the need for cognitive transformation in which ex-offenders are able to describe a coherent and new identity for themselves that accounts for and understands their criminal pasts. A credible story will therefore contain a more adaptive narrative identity that includes the idea of agency, flexibility and change; crucially, it needs to be a story that can also be persuasive in the eyes of others. In order to be persuasive – in our view – it must be owned by the offender, and it may also contain necessary shame-avoiding techniques that enable an individual to think that '*that was then, and this is now.*' Maruna refers to ways in which desisters recast their offending pasts not as shameful failings but as a necessary point in their transformation into something better. The offender also needs to be able to tell this story, with some fluency and conviction, even in the face of possible scepticism; we find that many ex-group members regress to their defensive states of mind when faced with a new and unconvinced audience – for example, a social worker investigating the welfare of his child – and are unable to demonstrate the genuine progress that they have made whilst in the group.

There are also ideas emerging from the literature on trauma and attachment that suggest that an individual's ability to offer a coherent sequential narrative about the past – without either negating the emotional impact, or being overwhelmed by it in the moment – is an indication of healthier processing of trauma and adversity.

We were attracted to Ryan and Lane's (1997) sexual assault cycle, which we adapted to suit our purposes, and it is laid out in Figure 5.1. The key task is to encourage the group member to link each section in their personal cycle in sequential order, whilst also taking a sufficiently flexible approach that allows for some offenders to emphasise one stage, and others another stage. It is important to remember that the redemptive narrative is that of the offender, not the preferred narrative of the therapists.

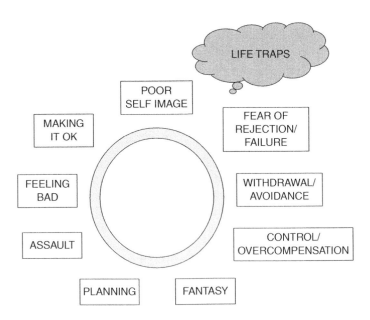

Figure 5.1 The sexual assault cycle

In summary, *poor self image* comprises relevant developmental experiences – often but not always adverse and potentially traumatic – that are formative; adolescent dating experiences and, in particular, the impact of puberty may also need to be taken into account. These experiences often result in life traps (schema) that have an impact on interpersonal relationships, particularly intimacy, and lead to a *fear of rejection, failure* or humiliation. Dysfunctional coping mechanisms can include either *withdrawal and avoidance* behaviours, or a tendency to become *controlling or to overcompensate*. Despite these coping methods bringing short term relief, they become increasingly unsatisfactory, as they seem to result in yet more difficulties in achieving closeness or connection to others. For some, imagination and use of the internal world (*fantasy*) becomes a substitute for relationships in the outside world, and a means of regulating how someone feels about themselves; this use of imagination can be a form of sexual coping, but for others, it might involve a longing for romance, or a desire for revenge (see Chapter 4 for more discussion of the role of fantasy). Tipping over into actual offending may occur suddenly for some, while for others a sequence of 'seemingly irrelevant decisions' or conscious *planning* may have taken place. Having committed the offences, individuals often *feel bad* about what they have done, even if this feeling is not well formulated, and a series of cognitive self-statements ensue with the purpose of dispelling lingering emotional discomfort, and *making it OK*.

Boxes 5.1 and 5.2 are slightly shortened narrative accounts from the cycle of two group members, articulated from their point of view, as they stand up before the other group members and 'tell my story.' Nick sexually assaulted his step-daughter over six months, but also has a prior conviction for grievous bodily harm on his first wife, and an adolescent conviction for indecent assault on a stranger he met at a party. Nick tended to emphasise his destructive side in a rather masochistic way, and for some time he became overly emotional when talking about his childhood, losing his way in the narrative; the facilitators worked hard to enable him to achieve a calmer and more balanced narrative that allowed discussion of his vulnerability and loneliness.

Box 5.1   Nick

My dad was a bastard, I hated him and what he did to me and my mum; she was so broken by him she had no love or time left for me. The sexual abuse taught me something else – I could control perverts,

(continued)

(continued)

make them desire me – and so I went out on the streets and used that power to get money. It was satisfying in a way (*poor self image*). Relationships, on the other hand, were dangerous, and I learnt it the hard way when my first love dumped me in the way she did; I know that I chose the bad ones after that – women I mean – because it was reassuring when they treated me badly, and I knew I was right not to trust them (*fear of rejection*). Drink was a way of avoiding everything, a sort of barrier between me and the world (*withdrawal*); but I was also scary and controlling, I know that now, I think my family was frightened of me, and that was how I wanted it (*controlling*).

Suzy (my partner) got that job in the pub, and that's when things really went down hill, as I knew this was the beginning of the end. I couldn't talk to her, and my drinking and rages got worse. I started to think about wanting to hurt her, how could I get revenge (*fantasy*), and that's when I started to think about hurting Tracey (my stepdaughter) – I wanted to destroy something that belonged to her, spoil it, show her how it hurt. It was easy of course, we were alone together a lot, and she was kind of scared of me (*planning*). Afterwards, I used to feel so bad about it that I stubbed out my fags on my arm (*feeling bad*), and the burns made me feel OK again. Tracey never said anything, it was easy to persuade myself that she was OK with it, although I don't think I really believed that, but I didn't care (*making it OK*).

John, on the other hand, had been highly resistant to thinking of his early life as anything other than 'normal,' and viewed his dismissal of any committed relationship as entirely justifiable. However, the facilitators were later able to engage with him in less shaming way – refraining from pointing out the emotional turbulence of his childhood, for example – and he was able to develop a cycle that emphasised some of his poor decision making around the offence.

Box 5.2   John

I don't know what the point of this is – my childhood was fine, and I don't think it's relevant. I was brought up by my gran – she spoilt me really and life was good. Dad was irrelevant, I met him when I was 14, but he had his own family and wasn't interested in us, and I certainly wasn't interested in him. I didn't really know my mum much – she had to work so hard to keep the family – and it was only when my gran died and I went back to live with mum that we had a sort of relationship (*poor self image*). I really objected to my step-dad trying to rein me in – now I can see that maybe I was angry, and he was doing his best – but at the time, I rebelled and ran wild. No one could tell me what to do, and I was out there, living the high life. I was hanging out with older guys, I learnt a trade – yeah it was illegal, but I had money, friends, and women.

There was never any problem with women, they liked me, I liked them, as long as there was no expectation (*fear of rejection*), no nagging (*withdrawal*), then things were fine. I've never been a violent guy, except when absolutely necessary, other guys taking the piss, that sort of thing (*controlling*). I'm not a rapist, I don't think that way. I don't know what happened that night when the offence happened. At the club, I preferred her friend but she was with my mate. The victim was OK though, she was high, I was high, we went back to my place and we had sex. The next day she was gone, I couldn't remember much, and the police only came along a month later.

It took me four years inside to re-think what happened, I resisted it, it made me uncomfortable (*feeling bad*). There were decisions I made, the crowd I was with, the way we thought about women . . . I think I expected to have sex that night (*planning*), and she was going to give it to me, nothing was going to stop me. It never occurred to me that she might have felt frightened (*making it OK*), but now I can see that I had more choices than she did.

The present: what presses my buttons

We work on the present – intimate, social and professional relationships and the problematic thoughts and feelings that they engender – at various points in the programme. We rely on mentalising ideas and techniques, but we teach the group members about schema modes and coping styles. We have a number of tasks that address the idea of 'thinking under pressure;' that is, when an individual's attachment issues have been activated. Despite individual differences, there are some regular problematic themes:

- Group members are preoccupied with third party disclosure concerns (discussed in more detail in Chapter 6), and although there is some considerable reality to their discomfort, underlying issues relate to a reactivation of humiliating and rejecting experiences in their earlier life, and the feelings of shame that are evoked with these fears are exposed.

- Group members are able to articulate two emotional states – angry and OK – and so a good deal of work is required to expand their ability to articulate and distinguish between more nuanced states of mind.
- Group members tend to hold narrowly rigid perspectives on the motives of others (in line with their mentalising difficulties) and a number of exercises and role plays are required to shift this style of appraising others.
- Group members tend to be either excessively compliant – and therefore say what they feel is expected of them – or deliberately oppositional. Tasks need to be sufficiently creative to enable group members to relax, and to speak their minds in a more reflective manner.
- Group members are quick to perceive the failings of others, often interpreted as persecutory and hostile attacks on them; and they expend considerable energy waiting for other people to change their behaviour. A key focus of the programme is to develop their ability to experience a sense of agency in changing how they interact with the world around them; that is, 'there are plenty of unreasonable people in the world, and you can't make them change, all you can do is change the way in which you deal with them.'

Practitioners will all have their own way of tackling these here and now difficulties. We encourage role play but have a rule that the facilitators must first expose their own anxieties about this by demonstrating scenarios and allowing a certain amount of personal humiliation. By lightening the mood and reducing the expectations of competence, there is likely to be far greater engagement. We often start with a more abstract, and therefore less threatening, exercise before targeting more personal difficulties that have direct significance for the group members. An example of this method, is the 'critical mum' scenario – and an extract from our manual is highlighted below.

> For example, an overcritical and demeaning mother talks with her adult daughter about her daughter's new boyfriend in a critical and somewhat rejecting/invalidating way. First, the daughter role plays an avoidant style of coping response; second she plays an over-compensating style; third, she plays a surrendering style. Finally, and with group input, she develops a healthy adult style in response to mother. At no time during the four 'takes' does the mother significantly alter her style of relating.
> (Challenge Project Manual, 2017)

Subsequently, group members are expected to bring live examples from the previous week, and they then link these examples to their learning about attachment styles, life traps and modes, and practice managing these situations whilst under pressure.

The future: knowing how risk may interfere with leading a 'good life'

Prior chapters have already touched on the problem for many sexual offenders when faced with negative lists of risk factors, and the way in which this feeds into their pre-existing perceptions of the world as a hostile place. The alacrity with which the GLM has been taken up is probably due to the positive response it receives from sexual offenders who value its strengths-based positively oriented approach.

Our view – in the absence of evidence-based guidance to say otherwise – is that the GLM needs to be more explicitly integrated with a risk model for optimum results. In our group programme, therefore, we try to address both. The GLM work probably resembles that which is undertaken widely and for all complexities of sexual offender. We find that many of our group members struggle with the abstract concepts of the primary goods and they tend to be highly avoidant of the small steps required to progress their GLM goals. Nevertheless, the most beneficial aspect of the GLM tasks is that it engages the offender and the facilitators in a collaborative narrative of hope, which in itself seems to engender agency within the offender.

It is worth articulating a little more clearly our approach to risk-related tasks within the group, as this could be perceived as slightly unconventional, and has been drawn from service user involvement work in the mental health services – and particularly non-forensic personality disorder services – within England and Wales (see for example, Haigh, Lovell, Lyon & Duggan, 2007; Jeffcote, van Gerko & Nicklin, 2018). Our aim is to empower the group members to understand and accept their risk, largely by means of sharing the knowledge base and by challenging each other to arrive at meaningful risk formulations. If we use the Risk Matrix 2000 and the Stable 2007 – which we do – then we must share those tools, and the associated knowledge about relative likelihood of sexual recidivism, with the group members.

We run this 'discuss your risk' task in the leaving session for each group member, an extract of which – from the manual – is shown below:

> The therapists should pass a paper and pencil around the group on which they must rate their view of the client's risk of re-offending. 0 represents no risk whatsoever, whilst 10 represents an absolutely certainty of re-offending. The ratings are written down by individuals privately, without discussion, and placed in a central container.

The facilitators should also complete this task. The scores are transcribed onto the flipchart and discussed. Group members are asked to identify which was their rating, and they are encouraged to explain the reasoning underpinning their ratings. Again, the facilitators participate equally in this task.

(Challenge Project Manual, 2017)

The aim of the task is not really to examine the probability ratings given by the group, but to explore each group member's thinking in relation to the leaving group member's risk, and how it reflects their thinking about themselves as well. It is important for the facilitators to be honest and informed in sharing their reasoning for the ratings. There is, of course, a tendency for individuals to be rated as 0, although sometimes group members are unexpectedly harsh on their peers.

In Chapter 2, we provided one example of how we have amended the Stable 2007 items to become service user friendly ratings, and we provide another example here (negative emotionality/hostility: see Figure 5.2). This self-rating task is part of a 'know your own risk' session which is also re-run in the Relapse Prevention two day programme. These ratings are then integrated into the group member's good lives oriented desistance plan for managing the future. This plan needs to be shared with the referrer, and any other relevant individual. We tend to articulate the small short term steps in the plan as well as the longer term aims, not least because many offenders with PPPD find it difficult to envisage a future that spans years rather than days.

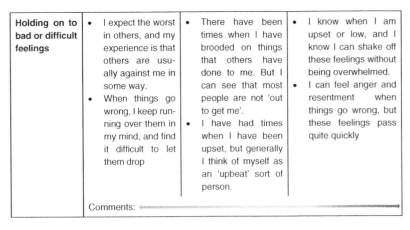

Holding on to bad or difficult feelings	• I expect the worst in others, and my experience is that others are usually against me in some way. • When things go wrong, I keep running over them in my mind, and find it difficult to let them drop	• There have been times when I have brooded on things that others have done to me. But I can see that most people are not 'out to get me'. • I have had times when I have been upset, but generally I think of myself as an 'upbeat' sort of person.	• I know when I am upset or low, and I know I can shake off these feelings without being overwhelmed. • I can feel anger and resentment when things go wrong, but these feelings pass quite quickly
Comments:			

Figure 5.2 Service user version of 'negative emotionality/hostility'

Summary

This chapter has attempted to collate the headline findings from the relevant evidence base for treating complex sexual offenders, and has provided some theoretical ideas and advice regarding the process and content of treatment. It is necessarily an overview of the key elements, but by no means definitive. The chapter concludes with a number of the most frequently asked questions regarding the practicalities of delivering community programmes for these challenging individuals; these, and our responses, are detailed in Table 5.1.

Table 5.1 Frequently asked questions and answers

Frequently asked questions	Answers
Is it better to have one female and one male facilitator?	It is nice to have a balance of genders as facilitators; however, on balance, it seems to make little difference to the group. Essentially, group members value facilitators for their honesty, likeability and experience. Sometimes, the facilitators feel compelled to take on stereotypical maternal/paternal roles within the group, and we attend to these dynamics very carefully.
How much training does a facilitator need?	We have chosen to use newly qualified psychologists, probation officers and other disciplines with a core mental health training. The main criteria for a good facilitator is an interpersonal style characterised by curiosity and warmth, with a degree of resilience in the face of defensive attitudes in offenders that can be enraging. Everything else can be taught, mostly in the course of weekly supervision.
How careful do you need to be with the composition of the group?	We used to say that a group of paedophiles is essentially a network; now we would add that a group of antisocial men is a gang, and a group of individuals with schizoid or avoidant traits is unbearably concrete and flat. The truth is that mixed groups work best, despite the tensions that arise as a result of widely divergent strengths and weaknesses; more than three of any one 'type' is probably ill-advised. Anyone too volatile to adhere to an implicit rule about no physical fighting is probably too disruptive for the group.

(continued)

Table 5.1 (continued)

Frequently asked questions	Answers
Is a group always more effective than individual treatment?	There is some evidence – albeit limited – to support the superiority of group work for sexual offenders generally. However, for those with PPPD, the interpersonal focus in group work is an important ingredient in the model of change. For the most part, sexual offenders prefer to avoid groups – we do not offer a choice for this reason – and we work with group members to develop a more compassionate and understanding perspective of their peers.
Are individual formulations for each group member necessary, or is the assessment of suitability sufficient?	We prefer to emphasise difference rather than similarity in the group; each group member needs to understand his area of risk, as well as his strengths. We encourage everyone to identify the areas that are most likely to lead to failure in their case. Without individual formulations, difficulties arise in the group process that are unexpected and challenging to manage; a formulation enables facilitators to identify potential dynamics before and as they emerge, and to attend to them before progress is sabotaged.
Do you set homework in-between sessions?	Most of our group members have had very aversive experiences of schooling, and expectations regarding homework trigger dysfunctional responses. Given that the group members rarely complete it, we prefer to avoid setting it, thereby reducing opportunities for confrontation and failure. This assists with improving our treatment completion, as we take the same stance with a range of other 'rules.'
How do you monitor the ban on socialising between group members outside the group session?	First, never set a rule that you cannot enforce. Second, our group members are so socially excluded and ostracised – and the evidence for socialising as a risk is not actually well established (except in rare organised crime networks) – that we allow peer support outside the group. Without encouraging it, we talk to group members about respecting each other's area of weakness; for example, not encouraging a peer to drink alcohol if it was implicated in their offending. Occasionally, this stance causes problems for us, but mostly, the group members forge supportive ties with each other.

Is it better for an offender to start the group immediately, or wait until he has settled down post-release?	On balance, our experience leans towards a preference to admit an offender to the group as soon as it possible following release from prison. Despite uncertainty regarding a range of social and personal issues, and high levels of anxiety, the structure of the group programme seems to offer stability and containment. We have found that delays tend to mean that the offender is more difficult to engage, resentful and avoidant.
How often do you change sessions around when they don't seem to work?	We have a rule: a particular group topic or task has to fail twice (over the course of two cycles of the programme) before we adjust it. Task failure can still take us by surprise but seems to be linked to uncertainty in the facilitators as to what the exact purpose of the task might be. Attending to facilitator understanding usually improves the engagement with the group members.
Do you permit the group to deviate from the manualised topic?	Although the manual is very specific about the tasks to be completed, there is flexibility regarding the time taken to achieve the task and an emphasis on combining the task with attention to the process. This enables facilitators to make some decisions about 'detours.' On balance, they are encouraged to keep up the pace of the group but to attend to process and group dynamics when these are relevant to the individual formulations, and/or when they threaten to interfere with task progress.

References

Andrews, D., Bonta, J. and Wormith, J. (2011). The risk-need-responsivity (RNR) model: Does adding the good lives model contribute to effective crime prevention? *Criminal Justice and Behavior*, 38, 735–55.

Bateman, A. and Fonagy, P. (2006). *Mentalization-based Treatment for Borderline Personality Disorder*. UK: Oxford University Press.

Bateman, A. and Tyrer, P. (2002). *Effective Management of Personality Disorder*. UK: Department of Health.

Bernstein, D., Nijman, H., Karos, K., Keulen-de Vos, M., de Vogel, V. and Lucker, T. (2012). Schema therapy for forensic patients with personality disorders: Design and preliminary findings of a multicentre randomized clinical trial in the Netherlands. *International Journal of Forensic Mental Health*, 11, 312–24.

Challenge Project Manual (2017). London: London Pathway Partnership and Psychological Approaches CIC.

Craissati, J. (2016). Therapeutic processes in sex offender treatment. In (ed.) D. Boer. *The Wiley Handbook on the Theories, Assessment, and Treatment of Sexual Offending* (pp. 421–32). Chichester: John Wiley & Sons Ltd.

Craissati, J. and Blundell, R. (2013). A community service for high-risk mentally disordered sex offenders: A follow up study. *Journal of Interpersonal Violence, 28,* 1178–200.

Craissati, J., South, R. and Bierer, K. (2009). Exploring the effectiveness of community sex offender treatment in relation to risk and re-offending. *Journal of Forensic Psychiatry & Psychology, 20,* 769–84.

Davidson, K., Halford, J., Kirkwood, L, Newton-Howes, G., Sharp, M. and Tata, P. (2010). CBT for violent men with antisocial personality disorder. Reflections on the experience of carrying out therapy in MASCOT, a pilot randomized controlled trial. *Personality and Mental Health, 4,* 59–162.

Dowsett, J. and Craissati, J. (2007). *Managing Personality Disordered Offenders in the Community: A Psychological Approach.* East Sussex: Routledge.

Fortune, C.A. and Ward, T. (2013). The rehabilitation of offenders: Striving for good lives, desistance, and risk reduction. In (ed.) J. Helfgott, *Criminal Psychology.* New York: Praeger Publishers.

Haigh, R., Lovell, K., Lyon, F. and Duggan, M. (2007). Service user involvement in the national PD development programme. *Mental Health Review Journal, 12,* 13–22.

Hanson, K., Bourgon, G., Helmus, L. and Hodgson, S. (2009). The principles of effective correctional treatment also apply to sexual offenders. *Criminal Justice and Behavior, 36,* 865–91.

Hopton, J., van Gerko, K. and Craissati, J. (2018). Evaluating sexual offenders in a community offender personality disorder programme. Forthcoming.

Jeffcote, N., van Gerko, K. and Nicklin, E. (2018). Meaningful Service User Participation in the Pathway. In (eds) C. Campbell and J. Craissati, *Managing Personality Disordered Offenders: A Pathway Approach.* Oxford: Oxford University Press.

Khan, O., Ferriter, M., Huband, N., Powney, M.J., Dennis, J.A. and Duggan, C. (2015). Pharmacological interventions for those who have sexually offended or are at risk of offending. *Cochrane Database of Systematic Reviews 2015, Issue 2.* Art. No.: CD007989. DOI: 10.1002/14651858.CD007989.pub2

Laws, R. and Ward, T. (2011). *Desistance from Sex Offending: Alternatives to Throwing Away the Keys.* New York: The Guilford Press.

Loesel, F. and Schmucker, M. (2005). The effectiveness of treatment for sexual offenders: A comprehensive meta-analysis. *Journal of Experimental Criminology, 1,* 117–46.

Malan, D. (1979). *Individual Psychotherapy and the Science of Psychodynamics.* London: Butterworths.

Mann, R. (1996). *Motivational Interviewing with Sex Offenders: A Practice Manual.* Hull: NOTA Publication.

Marques, J., Weideranders, M., Day, D., Nelson, C. and van Ommeren, A. (2005). Effects of a relapse prevention program on sexual recidivism: Final results from California's Sex Offender Treatment and Evaluation Project (SOTEP). *Sexual Abuse: A Journal of Research and Treatment, 17,* 79–107.

Marshall, W. and Marshall, L. (2009). *Treating Sexual Offenders: An Integrated Approach.* New York: Routledge.

Marshall, W. and Marshall, L. (2016). The treatment of adult male sex offenders. In (ed.) D. Boer, *The Wiley Handbook on the Theories, Assessment, and Treatment of Sexual Offending Vol. I* (pp. 1227–43). Chichester: John Wiley & Sons Ltd.

Maruna, S. (2001). *Making Good: How Ex-convicts Reform and Rebuild their Lives.* Washington, DC: American Psychological Association.

McAnena, C., Craissati, J. and Southgate, K. (2016). Exploring the role of locus of control in sex offender treatment. *Journal of Sexual Aggression, 22,* 95–106.

McMurran, M. and Theodosi, E. (2007). Is treatment non-completion associated with increased reconviction over no treatment? *Psychology, Crime and Law, 13,* 333–43.

Mews, A., di Bella, L. and Purver, M. (2017). *Impact Evaluation of the Prison-based Core Sex Offender Treatment Programme.* Ministry of Justice Analytical Series. London: Ministry of Justice.

O'Farrell, T., Fals-Stewart, W., Murphy, C., Stephan, S. and Murphy, M. (2004). Partner violence before and after couples-based alcoholism treatment for male alcoholic patients: The role of treatment involvement and abstinence. *Journal of Consulting and Clinical Psychology, 72,* 202–17.

Olver, M. (2016). The risk-need-responsivity model: Applications to sex offender treatment. In (ed.) D. Boer, *The Wiley Handbook on the Theories, Assessment, and Treatment of Sexual Offending Vol. I* (pp. 1227–43). Chichester: John Wiley & Sons Ltd.

Pfafflin, F., Bohmer, M., Cornehl, S. and Mergenthaler, E. (2005). What happens in therapy with sexual offenders? A model of process research. *Sexual Abuse: A Journal of Research and Treatment, 17,* 141–51.

Ryan, G. and Lane, S. (eds). (1997). *Juvenile Sexual Offending: Causes, Consequences and Correction* (2nd ed.). San Francisco: Jossey-Bass.

Stinson, J. and Becker, J. (2018). *Treating Sex Offenders: An Evidence-Based Manual.* New York: The Guilford Press.

Thibaut, F., de la Barra, F., Gordon, H., Cosyns, P., Bradford, J. and the WFSBP Task Force on Sexual Disorders. (2010). The world federation of societies of biological psychiatry (WFSBP) guidelines for the biological treatment of paraphilias. *The World Journal of Biological Psychiatry, 11,* 604–55.

Ward, T. and Keenan, T. (1999). Child molesters' implicit theories. *Journal of Interpersonal Violence, 14,* 821–38.

Ward, T., Yates, P. and Willis, G. (2012). The good lives model and the risk need responsivity model: A critical response to Andrews, Bonta, and Wormith (2011). *Criminal Justice and Behavior, 39,* 94–110.

6 Desistance and the art of giving up offending behaviour

Seeking social and human capital in a risk averse world

Introduction

In Chapter 5, it was made clear that treatment was only one possible component of a more wide-ranging toolkit of interventions and approaches to the management of sexual offenders; approaches that could broadly be described as psychologically informed. This chapter aims to explore those approaches in more detail, starting with ideas of desistance that have largely been driven by criminologists and then incorporating more psychologically driven ideas relating to attachment theory and pervasive psychological and interpersonal difficulties. The chapter will consider these ideas in relation to some of the most prevalent management approaches for sexual offenders in the UK and the USA; the question is whether traditional and, to some extent, common sense risk management approaches are consistent with or antithetical to emerging ideas about how complex sexual offenders may learn to desist from offending.

Understanding desistance

Desistance is an attractive theory for thinking about high risk repeat sexual offenders: as Chapter 2 clearly articulated, once convicted, the majority of sexual offenders pose a low risk of sexual recidivism; and we are therefore particularly exercised to understand the mechanisms by which a high risk offender decides or learns to give up his repetitive offending behaviours. If everyone (or almost everyone) gives up offending eventually, then the only questions he has to answer are when and how is he intending to give up, and whether there is something constructively helpful that we can do to ensure this process is as fast and effective as possible.

At first glance, it is easy to define desistance: the cessation of offending or other antisocial behaviour. However attempts to operationalise the concept have been more fraught – is it the absence of probation violations, new arrests or new convictions? At what point can an individual be thought to be desisting; one year or one decade after his last conviction? Probably the most useful approach is to consider desistance as a process – one that entails a potentially bumpy path in the direction of a persistently pro-social life – so this might entail consideration of longer periods of offence-free behaviour and less harmful acts as both being of relevance to desistance, as well as no further convictions. McNeill, Farrall, Lightowler and Maruna (2012) refer to the need for probation supervision to be realistic about the obstacles to desistance and to find ways to manage the setbacks and difficulties constructively.

No explanation of desistance is complete without a mention of two key pieces of criminological research. First, Glueck and Glueck (1950) studied the differences between 500 officially delinquent boys in America, matching them to 500 nondelinquents, all of whom lived in communities of relative social deprivation; they followed them up for ten years, and then again a further ten years later. Second, Sampson and Laub (1993, 2003) reconstructed and analyzed the Glueck data, and then obtained further follow up data on the participants up to the age of 70. They found that life-course desistance was normative for everyone, including all crimes; they emphasised 'turning points' such as marriage or a good job that led to the re-evaluation of a person's life, as well as the importance of human agency and choice in constructing new avenues of behaviour. These ideas were subsequently elaborated by Maruna (2001) in his Liverpool Desistance Study: Maruna found that whilst persisters developed condemnation scripts – seeing themselves as helpless, dependent on circumstances and as victims of society – desisters developed redemption scripts containing optimistic perceptions of themselves and their ability to control their lives and give something back. Maruna places more emphasis on this cognitive transformation than on the turning points of Sampson and Laub; cognitive transformation is described in more detail in Chapter 5 when discussing the sexual assault cycle (pp. 119–121). Closely related to this is the 'Pygmalion Effect' (cited in Laws & Ward, 2011, p. 58): that is, the high expectations of others leading to greater self-belief in the offender, such that rehabilitation can be thought of as an interaction between an individual and the relationships that are wrapped around him.

This idea of a reciprocal relationship between the offender and his social world is contained within the term social capital; that is, the ability of individuals to secure benefits (in Good Lives Model terms, primary goods) by virtue of membership in social networks and other social structures, realised through relationships (Wilson, 2014).

Resources that are possessed by the individual (such as capacities and skills) are often referred to as human capital. The characteristics of relationships that facilitate social capital have been described as 'shared norms, obligations, reciprocity, trust, rewards and sanctions' (Wilson, 2014, p. 64).

Research on sexual offenders and desistance

The very limited evaluation in this area is summarised in Milner (2016). The studies can, to a large extent, be criticised for their failure to distinguish desistance from a risk prediction model – for example, comparing those with higher risk profiles to those with lower risk profiles in relation to dynamic variables and reviewing outcomes – and for their failure to acknowledge that the majority of sexual offenders apparently stop offending after their first sexual conviction. Not unreasonably, such studies find that the shock of arrest, and associated feelings of shame, seem to be key influencing factors (Farmer, McAlinden, & Maruna, 2015), rather than issues of agency and social capital.

Implications for maximising opportunities for desistance

In summary, the implications of desistance theory for managing high risk sexual offenders seem to suggest that interventions should consider the following:

- Anticipate the lapses and relapses inherent in desisting, and manage them constructively
- Promote agency in a context of hope and optimism within the supervisory relationship and in relation to the offender's other social relationships
- Encourage cognitive transformation in the form of redemptive narratives that develop meaningful accounts of the shift from a previous offending self to an aspirational pro-social self
- Support opportunities for engagement with social capital that have the characteristics of reciprocity, shared values and the carrying out of mutual obligations.

Thinking psychologically about management approaches

Psychologically informed management approaches mean, in essence, that practitioners are mindful of their interactions with the sexual offender, consider the sentence/care plan, and organise the environment in which the offender is contained, in such a way as to best meet the offender's hypothesised emotional and psychological needs. These are therefore less exclusively individually focused and more relationally focused, and draw on psychological models of understanding human behaviour. In the case of complex sexual offenders – as defined in this book – they will integrate theoretical ideas about the development of persistent and pervasive psychological difficulties (PPPD) with an understanding of risk, sexualisation and desistance.

There are a range of models for thinking about psychologically informed management approaches, but I focus on three ideas here – all overlapping – that have informed my own practice and been found to be helpful by criminal justice staff (for more information, see Craissati, Joseph & Skett, 2015, pp. 68–78).

Attachment triangles

In Chapter 3, I proposed the use of attachment triangles to help with the development of an understanding of the offence in the context of an offender's relevant life experiences. The diagrammatic representation of this model is repeated here (see Figure 6.1), but now I propose that we extend this understanding to develop an anticipation of the likely behaviours that might be triggered in the context of the offender's relationship with his offender manager (probation) or police officer, and with his relationships in the current moment – as described in Chapter 5, the relational situations that 'press my buttons.'

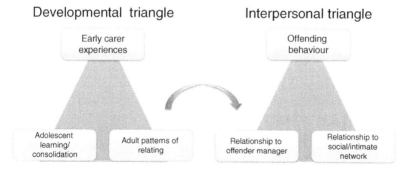

Figure 6.1 Formulating with triangles

Davies (1996, p. 133) describes this beautifully, and I quote him below:

> The view is taken that professionals who deal with offenders are not free agents but potential actors who have been assigned roles in the individual offender's own re-enactment of their internal world drama. The professionals have the choice not to perform but they can only make this choice when they have a good idea of what the role is they are trying to avoid. Until they can work this out, they are likely to be drawn into the play, unwittingly, and therefore not unwillingly. Because of the latter, if the pressure to play is not anticipated then the professional will believe he is in a role of his choosing. Unfortunately, initially, only a preview of the plot is available in the somewhat cryptic form of the offence . . . It is also important to comment that it is not only the offender's internal drama that professionals are called upon to enact but also those more explicit scripts of their own organisations and central government. They will also be under pressure from themselves to re-enact their own dramas.

Schemas and PPPD

For those who are more familiar or comfortable with psychological models that draw on cognitive behavioural ideas rather than psychodynamic terminology, both Millon and Padesky have operationalised the core and interpersonal characteristics associated with problematic personality types, integrated here in Table 6.1 (Craissati *et al.*, 2015) for simplicity.

Self-schema relates to the individual's core belief about himself, usually drawn from early developmental experiences and/or inherent traits, and reinforced over the years. *World schemas* describe the key traits with which the individual views himself in relation to the world around him/her. *Expressive acts* refer to the way in which others experience the individual with PPPD, the observable behaviours; and the *interpersonal strategy* describes the primary means by which the individual approaches and relates to others.

Whilst psychodynamic ideas may be endlessly nuanced but potentially inaccessible, cognitive ideas in relation to schema could be viewed, arguably, as excessively concrete and simplistic. An ability to move between the two theoretical positions – something that lies at the heart of integrative models – is perhaps the ideal.

Mentalising states of mind

The mentalisation based therapy model was described in Chapter 5, but is re-visited here simply to think about the importance of states of mind. By this I mean that within the practitioner-offender relationship there

Table 6.1 Schemas and personality characteristics (adapted from Craissati et al., 2015)

Personality type	Self-schema	World schema	Expressive acts	Interpersonal strategy
Paranoid	Right/noble	Malicious	Defensive	Suspicious or provocative
Schizoid	Self-sufficient	Intrusive or unimportant	Impassive	Isolated or unengaged
Schizotypal	Estranged	Variable	Eccentric	Secretive
Antisocial	Strong/alone	A jungle	Impulsive	Deceive or manipulate
Borderline	Bad or vulnerable	Dangerous	Spasmodic	Attack or attack
Histrionic	Inadequate	Seducible	Dramatic	Charm or seek attention
Narcissistic	Admirable	Threatening	Haughty	Compete or exploit
Avoidant	Worthless	Critical	Fretful	Avoid
Dependent	Helpless	Overwhelming	Incompetent	Submit
Obsessive–compulsive	Competent or conscientious	Needs order	Disciplined	Controlling or respectful

are, essentially, four states of mind and these are diagrammatically represented in Figure 6.2. Whilst the offender may or may not be aware of two of these states – knowing what is in his own mind and knowing also what he thinks is in the mind of the practitioner – it is the job of the practitioner to be curious about the four states of mind: what he/she is thinking, and what he thinks the offender is thinking, but also to anticipate and then to explore what the offender actually is thinking and how the offender might be thinking about the practitioner!

This capacity to consider the states of mind of oneself and others is an important ingredient, particularly in establishing a working relationship between the practitioner and the offender; the offender brings all kinds of assumptions into this relationship, and a wrong move early on can impede progress.

Let us return to the provisional formulations (see Box 6.1) for George and Simon (Chapter 3, pp. 77–81) and develop them a little further to consider what we might expect from them as they are (let us assume) discharged back into the community. If we think of **George** in terms of schemas, then we know that he has presented with the core characteristics of the antisocial and paranoid types of individual, although

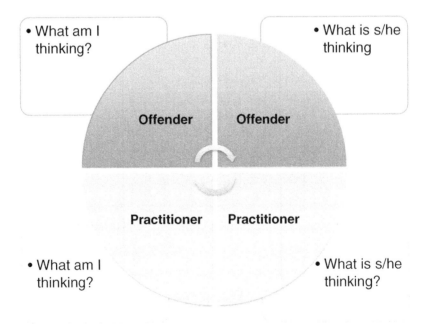

Figure 6.2 Four states of mind

it does seem that many of the impulsive behaviours associated with an antisocial lifestyle have dissipated over the years in prison and we are less likely to see rule breaking behaviours now. Furthermore, in my experience, individuals who display rather persecutory interpersonal styles in closed environments, often function better in the less toxic context of the community. Nevertheless, we might anticipate that George will present as fiercely independent, and confident in his own conclusions about the behaviours and motives of others as largely hostile, potentially malicious. We might expect him to be defensive, perhaps rather guarded, and although he may be superficially compliant, he is unlikely to be confiding or help-seeking. The rule of thumb here, is to avoid direct challenge to the core self-schema, but to engage with the individual offender – and indeed, to organise the management plan – in a way that circumvents these issues. For example, George is likely to be very resistant to attempts to empathise with him, or to appeal to his vulnerable side; he will be immediately suspicious of any note taking within a session or ask to see copies of previous reports and other interactions with a wider group of professionals. He may well refuse to talk about his childhood, or to give permission for practitioners to contact key family members; he will resent multiple and intrusive (as he perceives it) rules and expectations whilst he is under supervision.

Box 6.1   Provisional formulation for George and Simon

George had a relatively secure upbringing for his first decade, although in reality there was a lack of warmth in his bond with his mother that left him feeling anxious, a feeling compounded by his potential humiliation at school when he struggled to perform academically. For this reason, his status as 'special' in the eyes of his grandmother was all the more significant; and therefore the trauma of her death, all the more devastating. This disruption to his attachments came at a crucial point in George's development: he hated the feeling of weakness that came with caring and loss. He therefore rejected dependency on others in favour of an exciting bond with male peers that had elements of the vague glamour associated with his unknown father; and that provided an opportunity to substitute status and material acquisitions for intimacy.

(continued)

(continued)

The sexual offences occurred within this context, and represented an opportunity for George to consolidate his self-image in relation to his male peers, and to emphasise his ability to 'take' from women rather than to 'need' them.

Simon experienced a very unsettled and abusive childhood in which an affectionate bond with his mother was associated with uncontained states of anxiety, and where the unpredictability of life led to a focus on immediate gratification as a means of survival. For Simon, being 'seduced' into an habitually sexually abusive relationship was associated with confusing but largely comforting feelings of being loved and attended to in ways that were predictable and therefore reassuring. For him, the key trauma was not the onset of sexual abuse but the sudden loss of his 'sexual family' – particularly his innocent friendship with the boy – at the point of his first conviction. Subsequent patterns of behaviour were characterised by frantic sexualised contact with others in which he sought to re-capture an idealised version of his childhood, interspersed with brief periods of intense emotional turmoil in which he engaged in dramatic but destructive efforts to try and contain overwhelming feelings of distress.

George's interpersonal style elicits understandable suspicions and exasperation in equal measure in practitioners, and there can be a tendency to respond in ways that exacerbate the situation – for example, bringing another co-worker into the room, or becoming more restrictive in order to re-establish control over the challenging offender. Remember, if we are thinking in terms of states of mind, George is likely to be thinking that he does not have any problems, and should best be left alone; whilst he assumes that the practitioner is untrustworthy and intends to catch him out in the way that those in authority 'always do.' You cannot assume that he will accept your benevolent intentions, and he will soon provoke in you the assumption that his state of mind is seeking to 'pull the wool over my eyes!'

A more comprehensive list of 'tips' is detailed in the Appendices to Craissati *et al.* (2015). However, in summary here,

- Develop trust slowly and earn it in the first instance by being practical and helpful.
- Ignore demeaning comments and hostility.

- Behave transparently, explain your thinking and your actions, share your notes, and apologise in advance for any failings (he is going to selectively attend to your mistakes and shortcomings).
- If it can be tolerated, empathise with the feelings associated with the offender's world view.
- Keep the management plan simple, not too many individuals involved, keep expectations and rules to a minimum.

We could think of **Simon** in terms of core characteristics associated with borderline (emotionally unstable) personality traits. However, if we continue the formulation of his difficulties in line with the attachment triangles, we can see that there may well be an exacerbation of his interpersonal difficulties and the ensuing chaos as he leaves the relatively containing – and rule-bound – environment of a prison. In essence, we might anticipate that Simon will seek out multiple and indiscriminate relationships, all of which will commence in a rather idealised and intense fashion, and which will in turn trigger overwhelming anxieties that are responded to with a sequence of crises and self harm, eventually sapping the goodwill of the practitioner network. Simon is unlikely to understand the different roles of the local practice nurse, the probation officer, the police officer, and the other hostel residents, indiscriminately moving between them with excessively disclosing and dramatic accounts of his internal state. Interspersed within this chaos is likely to be some evidence of sexualised behaviour, as Simon falls back upon well tried patterns for self-soothing in terms of his ability to seduce others. This may, of course, take the form of sexual relationships within the probation hostel, or a period of prostitution. However, in my experience, practitioners can also be drawn into a 'rescuing' role, sometimes to the point of violating their normal working boundaries, and this may feed Simon's craving to be noticed and 'cared for'. Inevitably such seduction results in rejection as the pejorative terminology of 'manipulative' and 'attention-seeking' starts to be used.

In terms of the best ways in which to manage Simon's potentially challenging presentation, there are probably some key steps to take, and these are closely aligned to Davies' (1996) description of the offender drama and the need to understand the assigned roles.

- Draw up the detailed plan before Simon is released, as the difficulties are likely to arise very quickly upon release.
- The main focus is to bring all the relevant practitioners in and share the understanding of what to expect, as far as is possible. Communication is key.

- Identify which one or two practitioners will have the closer relationship with Simon and ensure that others keep their interventions more distant.
- Manage Simon's attachment needs by offering structured regular but time limited contact, and ensure that he is 'held in mind' when settled, rather than focusing attention on the periods of drama.
- Supervision is an important ingredient in helping the practitioners to ensure that they develop a warm relationship with the offender that remains within acceptable boundaries.
- Focus on the emotional experience, not the behaviour, and validate that experience no matter what your subjective view may be.

Current management approaches

Before returning to ideas of psychologically informed management and desistance later in this chapter, I want to examine the key sexual offender-specific management approaches that are prevalent in the UK and the USA at the moment and to consider the evidence base for their effectiveness. There are broadly five psychologically-relevant management approaches for sexual offenders in the community that are of particular salience:

1   Multi-agency public protection arrangements (MAPPA)
2   Procedures relating to sexual offender notification and third party disclosure
3   Circles of Support and Accountability
4   The polygraph
5   The offender personality disorder pathway (OPD pathway).

Multi-Agency Public Protection Arrangements (MAPPA)

In terms of Criminal Justice approaches, the most significant development in the community management of offenders in recent years in England and Wales is probably the development of Multi-agency Public Protection Arrangements (MAPPA). MAPPA was introduced in England and Wales in 2001 under the Criminal Justice and Court Services Act (2000, section 67 and 68) to facilitate the sharing of information among agencies to improve public protection. Police, Probation and Prison services form the Responsible Authority with a statutory duty to ensure that the risks posed by specified sexual and violent offenders are assessed and managed appropriately and other agencies – such as health, youth justice and the local authority – have a 'duty to co-operate' (Criminal Justice Act, 2003, section 325(3)).

MAPPA is not a stand-alone integrated management team, but represents innovative partnership working which appears to be making a contribution to reducing sexual and violent reconviction rates (Peck, 2011). The vast majority of complex high risk sexual offenders will be subject to MAPPA once out in the community, largely on account of being on the Sex Offender Register (Category 1), although a few might fall under Category 3 – any other dangerous offender. Sexual offenders can be managed at three levels: level 1 is when a single agency is involved and/or the risk management plan is straightforward; level 2 is for those who require multi-agency decision making and coordinated actions; and level 3 is for the critical few who are deemed to pose an immediate risk to others and/or may attract considerable public interest upon their release.

Examples of MAPPA annual reports can be found on the government website and you can see that the London report identifies 62% of all MAPPA offenders as Registered Sex Offenders, of whom 99% were managed at Level 1. Early evaluations of MAPPA were descriptive (see Dowsett & Craissati, 2007, for more detail) and process focused; there has been no convincing publication of any MAPPA evaluation that is able to demonstrate an effective impact on sexual recidivism.

In the USA, sex offender registration commenced as early as 1947 in California, but this became a requirement for all states with the Jacob Wetterling Act of 1994. A summary of research on the impact of registration on sexual recidivism suggests that there has been no impact on outcomes (Prescott & Rockoff, 2011); furthermore failure to register also does not appear to be associated with any significant increase in sexual recidivism. Given that the majority of studies have combined registration with notification, more details on this evidence base are referred to in the section below.

Procedures relating to sexual offender notification and third party disclosure

In the USA, two years after the 1994 Act, Megan's Law (1996) was enacted in New Jersey, and subsequently became a federal law: it was essentially argued that registration was insufficient, and community notification needed to be mandated. Subsequently, with the Adam Walsh Act of 2006, the Sex Offender Registration and Notification Act was widened to incorporate a greater number of offences and to include certain classes of adolescent sexual offender. Interestingly, previous methods of distinguishing between high and low risk offenders on the basis of risk classification tools were dropped; instead, distinctions were made solely on the basis of the index offence, and states are allowed to exceed the minimum requirements. Public notification – usually via a range of media – is also rather variable, with some states disclosing information only on the highest risk offenders, and others disclosing for all tiers of offender.

There is a helpful website summarising the evidence base for notification in the USA (Office of Sex Offender Sentencing, Monitoring, Apprehending, Registering, and Tracking, SMART). The impact of registration combined with notification has been very varied, with some states reporting a reduction and others an increase in sexual recidivism as a result; much seems to depend upon the methodology employed, and inconsistent allocation of sexual offenders to notification tiers (summarised in Lobanov-Rostovsky, 2015). Surveys of the public attitude to notification tend to report positive responses and offenders, when surveyed, often felt notification was a deterrent to recidivism. However, a large number of studies highlighted the negative impact of notification requirements on sexual offenders in terms of work, housing, harassment and disadvantage (cited in Lobanov-Rostovsky, 2015).

In the UK, notification was introduced later and rather more cautiously. In 2007, the Review of the Protection of Children from Sex Offenders was published which led to the Child Sex Offender Disclosure Scheme. The scheme is primarily the responsibility of the police, who manage a clear access route for the public to register their child protection interest in a named individual and – should there be relevant convictions and a risk posed – to receive a disclosure of pertinent information regarding the individual. There have been descriptive evaluations of the scheme (Chan, Homes, Murray & Treanor, 2010; Kemshall & Wood, 2010; Kemshall, Kelly & Wilkinson, 2012). The pilots resulted in a small number of enquiries being made, approximately 50% of which were taken further and 20% of which involved disclosure to a parent regarding the offender's conviction. In the 2012 study, applicants to the scheme were interviewed and, interestingly, those who were not in a professional role remained anxious as a result of the disclosure and uncertain as to how to make use of the information.

Disclosure (MoJ, 2012) – the sharing of specific information about a MAPPA offender with a third party (not involved in MAPPA) for the purpose of protecting the public – is considered to be an important and necessary resource for effective risk management of high risk sexual offenders. Intuitively this seems right, but it is an area that has been poorly evaluated. The MAPPA Guidance sets out principles underpinning the use of disclosure – that it should be lawful, proportionate, accurate and necessary – and provides advice around the decision to disclose. For example, it may be more appropriate to disclose information regarding key triggers rather than a list of offences; there may be viable alternatives to disclosure; advice should be offered regarding management. The guidance recommends that the offender knows that disclosure is taking place and that he has the chance to make the disclosure himself in the presence of the police or probation officer.

Penny and Craissati (2012) surveyed regular participants in MAPPA multi-agency meetings across London, with a response rate of 196 (61%): respondents expressed confidence in their knowledge of disclosure law and procedures but in fact held widely divergent views in their response to a range of hypothetical disclosure scenarios; and they held incorrect beliefs concerning the public's 'right to know.' A subsequent more detailed evaluation of disclosure within MAPPA (Craissati & Quarty, 2016) explored the nature and frequency of disclosures with reference to the methods used, the outcomes and subsequent offence failures. The study found the following:

- About 8% of all registered sex offenders had been subject to third party disclosure over the preceding 12 months, and around 50% of these were low to medium risk offenders as measured by the Risk Matrix 2000.
- It was far more common for a child sexual offender to be subjected to a disclosure rather than an offender whose victims were adults.
- The most common method of disclosure was for the police to telephone the recipient or to visit; most disclosures were to those in some sort of relationship with the offender.
- In terms of disclosures to employers, 65% of offenders were rejected as a result of disclosure; 40% were rejected by churches and housing providers following on from the disclosure. However, in terms of relationships (where proportionally more offenders were able to make the disclosure first), only 29% of offenders were rejected.

We know from the work in the Challenge Project that sexual offenders fear disclosure. Studies from the offender perspective (Connor, 2007; Hudson, 2005) suggest that offenders avoid situations potentially requiring disclosure for fear of rejection and retaliation; the offenders had already constructed personal narratives around their offending which avoided stigma – minimising or lying – which disclosure threatened, not least because of a fear of losing control over the disclosure process and it being used against them.

Circles of Support and Accountability (COSA)

The most creative innovations in recent years have arguably emerged from voluntary sector organisations; for example, the expansion of Circles of Support and Accountability (COSA) from delivery in small areas in rural North America to an established international presence, including increasing availability in the UK. A recent systematic review (Clarke, Brown & Vollm, 2015) provides a very good overview of the model and associated evaluations. Circles were first developed in Canada in the mid 1990s based on the principles of restorative justice (Bates, Macrae, Williams & Webb, 2011). They began as an informal community response to fears evoked by the release of high risk child sex offenders into the community, where individuals, mainly from the Mennonite Church, formed small groups or 'circles' around the released offenders. COSA aims to promote community integration of offenders by helping them develop and maintain engagement in positive activities and supportive relationships within the community. There are currently around ten COSA projects in England and Wales. A descriptive study of a well-established UK Circle, covering an eight year period, reported one sexual reconviction among the 60 core members reviewed (Wilson, Picheca, Prinzo & Cortoni, 2007). In addition, 70% of the sample attributed improvements in well-being to the support they received from their 'circle.' In a series of controlled studies based in Canada, it was found that involvement in a 'circle' suggested a reduction in general reconviction rates among those assessed as most likely to re-offend sexually. However, studies have been hampered by low base rates for sexual recidivism, small sample sizes, and short follow up periods. Clarke *et al.* (2015) concluded that overall there were few differences in the sexual recidivism rates between Circle members and matched controls; there was qualitative data to suggest improvements in the psychosocial functioning of members but limited quantitative data in this area. However, there appears to be modest evidence, in terms of cost-benefit analyses, of the costs being outweighed by the benefits.

Although COSA has restricted its remit to child sex offenders, some community projects for high risk personality disordered offenders have been heavily influenced by the model and have adapted it to work with those with adult victims and histories of physical violence. A preliminary mixed method evaluation of one example – Sova Support Link (SOVA – a UK charity that uses volunteers to support offenders) – demonstrated high levels of service user and referrer satisfaction with the service, high levels of engagement, and modest improvements in psychosocial functioning. This service was compared to a resettlement project with an identical ethos (the former delivering the service with volunteers, and the latter with paid social care staff), in terms of a service user perspective and found that there were similar levels of satisfaction and community integration with both models (Ward & Attwell, 2014).

The polygraph

There is perhaps nothing more likely to provoke heated debate and divergent views among practitioners than the question of the polygraph in relation to the post sentence management of sexual offenders. This debate is discussed in detail in Grubin (2016), as is the evidence to support its use. In the UK, the Offender Management Act 2007 sets out the statutory position regarding the mandatory testing of sexual offenders on parole; following pilot evaluations, from 2014 onwards, those who have served at least one year in prison and are deemed to pose a high risk of recidivism are subject to six monthly testing on release. In North America, the position is less clear: whilst such testing is hardly used in Canada, in the USA, it has been more widely used although the Federal 9th Circuit Appeal Court (cited in Grubin, 2016) ruled that an offender could not be compelled to waive his Fifth Amendment rights (against self-incrimination) and take a polygraph exam with the threat of prison recall if he did not.

In England the polygraphy tests have focused primarily on compliance with the terms and conditions of probation or parole, although tests may take place when there is a concern that an offender may have breached a licence condition or reoffended. In probation trials, over 90% of offender managers rated polygraphy as being helpful, and none considered it to have a negative impact. However, this is not the same as concluding that polygraphy results have improved treatment outcomes or genuinely reduced sexual recidivism.

There have been two UK studies that have examined the efficacy of polygraphy in facilitating relevant disclosures in comparison with a contemporaneous group of offenders with whom polygraphy is not used. The first trial was voluntary and the second mandatory, and both confirmed that the use of polygraphy was associated with greatly increased odds of making relevant disclosures. Interestingly, whilst 73% of interviewed probation officers believed the offenders they supervised were open with them, this was the case for only 25% of those who supervised polygraphed offenders.

There is an error rate with polygraphy, with a variety of studies finding similar results – an error rate of 10–20% – and a suggestion that those who falsely disclose (false positives) have the same characteristics as those who make false confessions in police interviews (higher scores on the NEO neuroticism scale and lower scores on the conscientiousness scale,

Grubin & Madsen, 2006). Because of this error rate, Grubin advises that the utility of polygraphy post-sentence needs to be emphasised rather than its accuracy, with disclosures being seen as more important than the test outcome itself. In the UK, a released offender cannot be recalled to prison on the basis of a 'failed' polygraphy test, although it is of course the case that if disclosures reveal significant breaches of release conditions (licence), then an offender will be recalled on that basis.

The error rate is one of the main criticisms of polygraphy, and is certainly a concern among those offenders with PPPD, some of whom may be particularly prone to making false confessions. There is also a prevalent myth among offenders that the polygraph is a 'lie detector' test and it may therefore be the case that they make disclosures in expectation of being 'found out.' Informing them in advance of the error rate is one recommended means of addressing this ethical issue. Grubin also points out the importance of ensuring that there is rigorous training and supervision of polygraph assessors to counter the very real risk otherwise of drift toward unethical practice.

The offender personality disorder (OPD) pathway

The OPD pathway strategy is specific to England and Wales, and is comprehensively described in a special edition of Criminal Behaviour and Mental Health (Skett, Goode & Barton, 2017) and in Campbell and Craissati (2018). In essence it operationalises many of the ideas put forward in Chapter 3. The strategy emerged as a result of learning from earlier programmes for the highest risk offenders with personality disorder that were predicated on intensive treatment approaches; as well as recognising the high prevalence of personality disorder among offenders, and limited evidence base for such individuals accessing meaningful and effective intervention programmes. The OPD pathway is a joint National offender Management Service (NOMS – now known as HMPPS – Her Majesty's Prison and Probation Service) and National Health Service (NHS) strategic initiative that targets adult offenders posing a high risk of harm to others and with persistent and pervasive psychological difficulties (PPPD) that may be indicative of personality disorder, although no diagnosis is required. Psychologically informed management lies at the heart of this unique approach and is reflected in:

- Joint criminal justice and mental health delivery at strategic, operational, and practitioner levels, thereby mirroring the presenting needs and challenges posed by complex offenders, and avoiding organisational conflict and fragmentation.

- A triage system for identifying those offenders most in need that is based on non-specialist but evidence based steps embedded within existing assessment systems, thereby increasing access to the service and locating it within the probation and prison services.
- A formulation-led approach to sentence planning for offenders with PPPD that emphasises the development of the workforce (rather than an exclusive focus on the offender), with a system of consultation, reflective practice and training.
- A focus on relational and environmental aspects of management at all points in the pathway, from community through prison and back into the community, with a very greatly reduced emphasis on the delivery of formal interventions and greatly increased accessibility for less 'psychologically-minded' offenders.
- Clarity regarding the expected high level outcomes, which include a reduction in sexual and violent offending, improved psychological well-being, greater confidence and competence in the workforce, and economic efficiency.

The strategic team have had the foresight to commission a national evaluation of the OPD pathway and results will be available later in 2018. However there are a number of smaller local evaluations that provide preliminary support for the approach taken in terms of: the ability of non-specialist staff to screen and triage, the benefits of workforce training, the impact of consultation, and greater access to opportunities to progress for offenders who were otherwise facing an impasse.

Psychologically informed risk management in action

The chapter, thus far, has set out in detail a range of approaches to the community management of complex high risk sexual offenders, some of which are more psychologically informed than others. It will already have become clear that there is a lack of hard evidence – admittedly such an evaluation task is challenging – that many (if any) of these approaches have been shown to have a significant impact on reducing the sexual recidivism rate. The reader may also have discerned that some of the more rigorous external controls seem to have the potential to contradict core desistance principles, despite intuitively appearing to be attractive measures.

In this section, I want to bring a more personal note to the question of psychologically informed risk management by sharing a few examples of offender and practitioner conversations that I have encountered – selected in an entirely biased way! – in order to bring alive the dilemmas involved in developing risk management that is meaningful and impactful.

Example 1: volunteers and SOVA Support Link (www. sova.org.uk/project/SupportLink)

(Volunteer) It's changed my perspective, working with Barry . . . I used to despise sexual offenders, what they do, you know . . . but now I can see behind the offences, and they are just people really, with problems and difficulties.

(Barry) I've had a psychologist, and therapy, you know . . . and she cared, but it wasn't the same, she was paid. With SOVA, I just can't believe that ordinary people would give up their time to help me, that's what really shocks me.

It may be that projects like SOVA, modelled on Circles of Support, struggle to demonstrate hard outcomes in terms of sexual recidivism; but it was conversations like these that made me realise the potential value of volunteers in terms of social capital and ideas of reciprocal relationships and community integration.

Example 2: third party disclosure and the 'psychology of the practitioner'

I was discussing a case with a police officer: the offender was a high risk repeat indecent exposer who offended against stranger women intermittently at times when his intimate relationships broke down. The police had disclosed his offence history to his new girlfriend and I was arguing that the disclosure may not have been proportionate given the partner was not at risk. The police officer responded with:

"Of course it's proportionate, he's a sexual offender and that makes it proportionate . . . She has a right to know." With some further discussion, he added "Would you want your daughter to move in with a convicted sex offender?"

Strictly speaking the police officer was wrong in his interpretation of the – admittedly vague – legal and statutory situation in England. But I was struck by his emotional honesty nevertheless, and recognised his view was shared by many if not most (including mental health professionals, Penny & Craissati, 2012), and was strongly driven by an understandable moral discomfort about knowing something and not passing it on. This emotional undercurrent is what is not discussed in the MoJ MAPPA Guidance (2012), and may be the dominant reason why such disclosures lead more often to rejection than to acceptance by the recipient (Craissati & Quarty, 2016). It seems that disclosure may be as much to do with moral as with public protection imperatives, with an emphasis on rights rather than responsibilities.

Example 3: psychologically informed management and offender engagement

Shaw, Higgins and Quartey (2017) randomly allocated probation staff to a case formulation group and treatment as usual group, and they were then randomly allocated high risk offenders with a personality disorder. The staff in the formulation condition were given training and then asked to construct collaborative case formulations with the offenders over a 12 week period. All participants subsequently completed a relationship quality scale and a perceived benefits rating scale. Staff in the formulation conditions reported significantly higher overall relationships quality, a stronger working alliance, and greater confidence. Offenders in the formulation group reported significantly higher degrees of trust in their probation officer.

This small project was hugely important in taking a step towards confirming our working hypothesis, that non psychologically trained staff, drawing on psychological ideas to influence their sentence plan, might be able to significantly improve the offender's compliance with and engagement in supervision.

Example 4: the challenge of cognitive transformation and risk management

(Greg). I was furious, he had never even met me, and I thought to myself . . . so he thinks I'm high risk, I'll show him what high risk means . . . I went out and bought a knife . . . on the way out I passed my relapse prevention plan stuck on the fridge. It said "Ring Jackie," but I decided to ignore it and went out anyway.

This salutary experience related to an offender who was released into the community after 20 years in prison, including a successful two year stay in Category D (open) prison where he had worked and enjoyed responsibility and freedom. He was stringently managed in the community, but maintained a positive approach until the week in which he went out and committed a serious further offence. When we were discussing the serious further offence afterwards in prison, it seemed to me that the triggers were very commonplace: he had had the not uncommon experience of handing over his disclosure letter to yet another potential employer, watching the man's face change and being told that he would be contacted in due course. He also asked to be downgraded in his risk level but although his probation officer was supportive of this, the area lead wanted to take a more cautious approach and maintain the status quo for a few more months. No one had acted unreasonably or without integrity; yet the experience for the offender was one of relentless condemnation, loss of hope, and – as he saw it – a rejection by others of his 'redemptive narrative' about himself and his offending. Of course, one interpretation might be that his subsequent actions confirmed what we should always have realised, that he was a high risk offender with the potential to reoffend; but this circular argument is somewhat limiting, as it does not enable us to reflect on how our actions may influence the path to desistance or to relapse.

Example 5: service user involvement as a source of social capital (Craissati, 2015)

(Peter) I sit on interview panels where we interview future volunteers . . . often the decision is 50% made by me which makes me feel a bit more enabled to give back . . . and I do a talk to potential volunteers . . . the benefits to me have had a big impact, because I have been analyzing myself and seeing where I am now and where I was before . . . I'm treated like a colleague . . . I actually feel quite . . . how can I say . . . I just feel honoured for the fact that I've been able to be part of the organisation in this way and I am able to give back something. I just feel honoured that they've asked me to be part of it.

(Ian) Well there are five of us (released sexual offenders) scattered around the countryside at the moment. We talk, we phone, we visit, and we generally keep in touch. If any of us have got any problems hopefully we phone each other and sort it out. Statistically we should have been in and out of prison two or three times – we haven't; if everybody had done what everybody says – paedophile rings springs to mind – God knows what would have happened to the five guys with no support.

Service user involvement has not developed within the sphere of sexual offender work, for reasons that are obvious in terms of risk. However, the literature on emotional loneliness and social isolation as dynamic risk concerns is fairly robust, whilst the research literature on sexual offender friendships leading to sexual recidivism is almost entirely absent except in those fairly rare cases of organised sexual offending in the index offence. Here you can glimpse the powerful impact that meaningful involvement can have on the offender's sense of self worth, and his sense of a reciprocal relationship with others, including other offenders.

Summary

With a falling sexual recidivism rate overall (see Chapter 1 for more details), it does seem right to conclude that MAPPA – and the rigorous risk management approach that underpins it – is playing a constructive role in this positive outcome. Public protection is, quite rightly, the first priority of any community risk management approach. Yet the evidence for any of these intuitively sound, rigorous approaches – information exchange, third party disclosure, polygraphy, community notification – significantly reducing the sexual recidivism rate is sadly absent. This is undoubtedly partly due to the difficulties in evaluating such interventions when the desired outcome is the absence of an event. However, in my view, it is also because these interventions seem so intuitively sound, that it does not always occur to us to question them, or indeed to take any notice of the absence of impact, when we do have such evidence.

What we do know is that the public is reassured by such external controls, far more than the evidence would support; that is, the public generally, for we also know that the individual recipients of disclosures remain anxious, uncertain, and more often than not, respond with exclusion of the offender from their midst.

The nagging question remains as to whether our target group – high risk, personality disordered sexual offenders – is in fact rendered more risky (or less likely to desist) in the context of stringent risk management approaches? That is, they are not simply more likely to be lonely, aggrieved, excluded, and deceitful – but risky behaviour is actually triggered as a result? Let us re-visit the four bullet points summarising the implications of desistance theory for high risk sexual offenders:

- Anticipate the lapses and relapses inherent in desisting and manage them constructively.
- Promote agency in a context of hope and optimism within the supervisory relationship and in relation to the offender's other social relationships.
- Encourage cognitive transformation in the form of redemptive narratives that develop meaningful accounts of the shift from a previous offending self to an aspirational pro-social self.
- Support opportunities for engagement with social capital that have the characteristics of reciprocity, shared values and the carrying out of mutual obligations.

For an offender whose childhood experiences have coloured his experience of relating to others in the here and now, and whose state of mind does not have access to our more rational reality testing, stringent risk management may trigger dysfunctional responses. These, in turn, may provoke punishing responses in ourselves, creating a downward spiral. Thoughts of third party disclosure may evoke overwhelming feelings of shame and humiliation and be managed by self-destructive avoidance (or secrecy); polygraphy may provoke a false confession in an attempt to please the interviewer; long lists of behaviour rules are broken with a delinquent resolve to test the reliability or predictability of the authority figure who has to police them; and exclusion from reciprocal social engagement opportunities creates an angry despondency and rejection of pro-social community norms.

Although it does appear to be the case that current approaches to risk management are potentially contrary to the principles of desistance, there are some encouraging signs of opportunities moving forward. We are learning that there may be considerable community value from volunteer participation in programmes to manage sexual offenders, and we are beginning to explore whether or not there may in fact be benefits to the service user holding a significant role in relation to peer support. There is also a modest but developing evidence base to suggest that attention to psychological ideas can inform risk management in such a way as to anticipate and circumvent obstacles to rehabilitation.

References

Bates, A., Macrae, R., Williams, D. and Webb, C. (2011). Ever- increasing circles: A descriptive study of Hampshire and Thames Valley Circles of Support and Accountability 2002–2009. *Journal of Sexual Aggression, 18*, 355–73.

Campbell, C. and Craissati, J. (2018). *Managing Personality Disordered Offenders: A Pathway Approach.* Oxford: Oxford University Press.

Chan, V., Homes, A., Murray, L. and Treanor, S. (2010). *Evaluation of the Sex Offender Community Disclosure Pilot.* Scotland: Ipsos MORI.

Clarke, M., Brown, S. and Vollm, B. (2015). Circles of support and accountability for sex offenders: A systematic review of outcomes. *Sexual Abuse: A Journal of Research and Treatment, 29*, 446–78.

Connor, J. (2007). *Disclosure of Sexual Offending: Offenders' Perspectives.* Doctoral thesis (Clinical Psychology): University of East London.

Craissati, J. (2015). Meaningful service user voices in the delivery of community sex offender services. *NOTA News, 76*, 17–19.

Craissati, J., Joseph, N. and Skett, S. (2015). *Working with Offenders with Personality Disorder: A Practitioners Guide (2nd Ed.).* National Offender Management Service & NHS England. (www.gov.uk).

Craissati, J. and Quarty, C. (2016). An exploration of third party disclosure and outcomes in registered sex offenders. *British Journal of Community Justice, 13*, 51–64.

Davies, R. (1996). The inter-disciplinary network and the internal world of the offender. In (eds) C. Cordess and M. Cox, *Forensic Psychotherapy: Crime, Psychodynamics and the Offender Patient* (pp. 133–44). London: Jessica Kingsley.

Dowsett, J. and Craissati, J. (2007). *Managing Personality Disordered Offenders in the Community: A Psychological Approach*. East Sussex: Routledge.

Farmer, M., McAlinden, A. and Maruna, S. (2015). Understanding desistance from sexual offending: A thematic review of research findings. *Probation Journal, 62*, 320–35.

Glueck, S. and Glueck, E. (1950). *Unraveling Juvenile Delinquency*. New York: Commonwealth Fund.

Grubin, D. (2016). Polygraph Testing of Sex Offenders. In (eds) R. Laws and W. O'Donohue. *Treatment of Sex Offenders: Strengths and Weaknesses in Assessment and Intervention* (pp. 133–56). Switzerland: Springer.

Grubin, D. and Madsen, L. (2006). Accuracy and utility of post-conviction polygraph testing of sex offenders. *British Journal of Psychiatry, 188*, 479–83.

Hudson, K. (2005). *Offending Identities. Sex Offenders' Perspectives on the Treatment and Management*. Devon, UK: Willan.

Kemshall, H., Kelly, G. and Wilkinson, B. (2012). Child Sex Offender Public Disclosure Scheme: The views of applicants using the English pilot disclosure scheme. *Journal of Sexual Aggression, 18*, 164–78.

Kemshall H., and Wood, J. (2010). *Child Sex Offender Review (CSOR) Public Disclosure Pilots: A Process Evaluation Research Report 32, Key Findings (2nd edition 2010)*. London: Home Office.

Laws, D. and Ward, T. (2011). *Desistance and Sex Offending: Alternatives to Throwing Away the Keys*. New York: Guilford Press.

Lobanov-Rostovsky, C. (2015). *Adult Sex Offender Management*. (http://www.smart.gov/pdfs/AdultSexOffenderManagement.pdf).

Maruna, S. (2001). *Making Good: How Ex-convicts Reform and Rebuild their Lives*. Washington, DC: American Psychological Association.

McNeill, F., Farrall, S., Lightowler, C. and Maruna, S. (2012). *How and Why People Stop Offending: Discovering Desistance*. Institute for Research and Innovation in Social Services. (http://eprints.gla.ac.uk/79860/)

Milner, R. (2016). *Desistance in Men Who Have Previously Committed Sexual Offences: An Exploration of the Early Processes*. PhD thesis: University of York, UK.

Ministry of Justice (2012). *MAPPA Guidance 2012 Version 4*. National Offender Management Service; Association of Chief Police Officers. (https://www.justice.gov.uk/downloads/offenders/mappa/mappa-guidance-2012-part1.pdf).

Ministry of Justice (2017): *MAPPA Annual Reports 2016-2017: Reports for Each Multi-Agency Public Protection Arrangements (MAPPA) Area for 2016 to 2017*. London UK: Ministry of Justice. (https://www.gov.uk/government/publications/mappa-annual-reports-2016-to-2017).

Peck, M. (2011). *Patterns of Reconviction Among Offenders Eligible for MAPPA*. London: Ministry of Justice.

Penny, C. and Craissati, J. (2012). Decisions on disclosure to third parties made at MAPP meetings: Opinions and practice. *The Psychiatrist, 36*, 379–85.

Prescott, J. and Rockoff, J. (2011). Do sex offender registration and notification laws affect criminal behavior? *Journal of Law and Economics*, *54*, 161–206.

Sampson, R. and Laub, J. (1993). *Crime in the Making: Pathways and Turning Points Through Life*. Cambridge, MA: Harvard University Press.

Sampson, R. and Laub, J. (2003). Life-course desisters? Trajectories of crime among delinquent boys followed to age 70. *Criminology*, *41*, 301–40.

Shaw, J., Higgins, C. and Quartey, C. (2017). The impact of collaborative case formulation with high risk offenders with personality disorder. *The Journal of Forensic Psychiatry & Psychology*, *28*, 777–89.

Skett, S., Goode, I. and Barton, S. (2017). A joint NHS and NOMS offender personality disorder pathway strategy: A perspective from 5 years of operation. *Criminal Behaviour and Mental Health*, *27*, 214–21.

Ward, M. and Attwell, P. (2014). Evaluation of two community outreach forensic psychological services. *Journal of Forensic Practice*, *16(4)*, 312–26.

Wilson, H. (2014). Criminal justice? Using a social capital theory to evaluate probation-managed drug policy. *Probation Journal*, *61*, 60–78.

Wilson, R., Picheca, J., Prinzo, M. and Cortoni, F. (2007). Circles of support and accountability: engaging community volunteers in the management of high-risk sexual offenders, *The Howard Journal*, *46*, 1–15.

7   Where are we now?

This brief chapter aims to summarise key learning points from the preceding chapters. The aim of the book has been to facilitate the very best practice among practitioners, mindful of the resource limitations and pressures that they face. The chapter draws together a ten-step model to reflect the steps necessary to achieve this best practice in the psychologically informed management of complex sexual offenders. In doing so, I hope to demonstrate how far we have come in the past two decades but also where our gaps in knowledge lie. I conclude with a rather personal take on the necessary ingredients for future success in this field.

A 10-step approach

Figure 7.1 outlines my proposed ten-step approach, ten being a somewhat arbitrary number of course but relatively easy to remember. Note that I commenced my view of complexity in this book with the chapter on risk assessment, as it seemed important to tackle the vexed question of low versus high risk sexual offenders early on in order to clear our thinking for more complex psychological ideas of personality difficulties and 'perversion.' However, in my proposed ten-step model, I commence with ideas around the 'why' (did the offence happen), rather than the 'whether' (he will do it again) as in an ideal world this is my preferred order of thinking about a sexual offender. However, the rights and wrongs of an approach depend on the practitioner and the context, and readers should feel free to consider the ten steps in a way that meets their needs.

Seek
- Bring a curious and relational focus to understanding the history & the offending
- Make no 'obvious' assumptions about links in the developmental pathway

Why
- Ensure the formulation is succinct, psychologically plausible, explanatory, & envisages 'next steps'
- The formulation should meet the recipients' needs & be owned by them, which is likely to mean it should be simple, short & confident

Static
- Note the base rate for offending, as well as allocating a relative risk category
- Low risk means light touch approach; high risk should never be forgotten

Dynamic
- This is about which of those in the risk category are more like to recidivate
- Remember you are looking for persistent traits, not offence specific ones
- Worry much more about sexual preoccupation & antisocial lifestyle/traits than intimacy or attitudes

Failures
- Note the exact reasons for all prior failures (including recall to prison), & the speed of failure
- Take into account the offender's view on past failures

Worry
- Consider the single factor most likely to tip the offender into offending (immediate trigger)
- Take into account the offender's primary concern about risk

Integrate
- Formulation & risk assessment, noting & focusing on the areas of overlap
- Disentangle personality traits that interfere with progress from traits that drive risk

Anticipate
- Likely short term failure including response to licence conditions/rules
- Multi agency/interpersonal dynamics
- And prepare others & yourself

Plan
- Role of treatment, whether & why it has a significant role to play, to what purpose & with what focus
- Ensure as much or more attention is paid to the wider approach to psychologically informed management

Test
- Is the plan in line with known evidence base & desistance theory?
- Never make a threat you're not prepared to carry out; discard all rules that are not central to risk
- Check the plan with the offender, to ensure his 'state of mind' is in tune with yours
- Do no harm!

Figure 7.1 A 10-step approach to managing complex sexual offenders

Step 1: Seek

Both Chapter 3 (personality disorder) and Chapter 4 ('perversion') emphasised the need to take a curious stance and explore the sexual offending behaviour in a relational context in which

- the offending has meaning in terms of intimacy
- the developmental pathway to offending is fluid and individualised
- biology, psychology and the social/cultural context are all relevant and interdependent.

In my view, we are at an exciting point at which our understanding of neurobiology is becoming consistent with our more recent understanding of effective approaches to working with persistent and pervasive psychological difficulties (PPPD); the evidence base suggests that it is futile to expend needless energy on arguing from the point of view of 'nature' or 'nurture,' as our model is now more coherently integrative. This integrative understanding enables us to understand why traumatic experiences of childhood sexual victimisation in one individual might influence their pathway to sexual offending whilst for many others the same experience might lead in a very different direction; and why, for many, their pathway to sexual offending may be less obviously driven by specific trauma experiences and more overtly variable and fluid than we might anticipate.

Step 2: Why

A formulation comprises the explanatory summary of step one and is described in Chapter 3 (as well as in more detail in Chapter 3 of the Ministry of Justice 2015 guide). It should be explicitly or implicitly collaborative and oriented towards recipients in order to meet their needs. It provides the basis for all future oriented hypotheses about relational aspects of the offender and we return to the formulation in step seven below. Our ability to evidence the impact of a good formulation on the outcome – reduced sexual recidivism – is not yet established and so we must treat the task with due caution. However, there are some emerging findings that suggest a formulation can build the confidence of the practitioner in managing a complex case (Knauer, Walker & Roberts, 2017) and that it can significantly improve the quality of engagement between the practitioner and the sexual offender (Shaw, Higgins, & Quartey, 2017), something that may well enhance compliance and thereby reduce recidivism risk.

Step 3: Static

Step 4: Dynamic

We now move away from the theoretically driven case formulation in order to focus on the empirically driven basis for risk assessment. Chapters 1 and 2 set the scene for acknowledging the relatively low sexual recidivism rate of sexual offenders; despite our awareness of the limitations around reconviction data, there is international evidence that sexual recidivism remains fairly low and is continuing to reduce in frequency to below 10% after four years at risk (Thornton & d'Orazio, 2016). In considering high risk offenders, the case is made in Chapter 2 for an objective and disciplined approach in which intuitive beliefs about risk have to be set aside in the light of robust evidence. Despite the popularity of structured professional judgement approaches, the evidence continues to favour actuarial approaches in terms of predictive accuracy. Furthermore, despite public scepticism regarding expertise in this area, and some heated debate within the field, I would suggest that we now have a more consistent and robustly evidence based understanding of relative risk in sexual offenders than we do in any other aspect of criminal justice and mental health.

Step 5: Failures

Step 6: Worry

Noting prior failures – particularly the triggers to failures other than sexual recidivism – entails adopting an approach akin to a functional analysis of behaviours, identifying antecedents and consequences. It is at this point that we are moving away from empiricism in relation to risk and our understanding of PPPD begins to merge with our thinking about risk. In the Challenge Project, for example, we found that factors associated with the risk domain of general self management (or PPPDs that were strongly antisocial and/or emotionally unstable) led to repeated failures, particularly impulsive decision making and persistently hostile attitudes towards supervision. These were not the same variables as those implicated in sexual recidivism. Engaging the sexual offender in a more collaborative exchange about risk and worry – what's on your mind, what's on my mind – begins to raise ideas about reciprocity, empowerment and agency in terms of desistance and next steps.

Step 7: Integrate

This is the pivotal moment in which all the information from the past – developmental, psychological and risk/offence-related – is brought together, integrated, and used as a springboard to a future oriented management plan. Chapters 3 and 4 have already identified the very considerable overlap between ideas of persistent and pervasive traits, with descriptions of dynamic domains; here we take a step further to identify the way in which PPPDs and risk factors interact with each other. The key task is to disentangle those traits and behaviours that are directly relevant in driving sexual and violent offending from those that 'get in the way by pressing our buttons' in terms of raising anxieties and negativity in practitioners, or that lead to impasse in an offender's progress.

Step 8: Anticipate

Step 9: Plan

In thinking about the future, it is helpful to separate out a fairly short term 'anticipatory' plan from a longer term risk management plan that focuses on sexual (and/or violent) recidivism. The former – akin to a crisis and contingency plan in mental health services – identifies, on the basis of step 7, immediate triggers to dysfunctional behaviours and sets out the expected interpersonal difficulties. As Davies' (1996, p. 136) described it, the nature of the play is identified, there is an outline of the plot, and each player knows the role that he is likely to have to play.

Treatment is one element of the plan, and Chapter 5 clearly outlines the potential focus of therapy and the expected mechanism of change. We are now increasingly clear as to what constitutes an effective treatment package in relation to PPPD but remain hampered by our need to engage what are often ambivalent individuals in a fairly sophisticated and verbally-oriented process of internal change. As with so many other mental health interventions, the majority of sexual offenders with PPPD either do not wish to access psychological treatment (they fail to survive the assessment or settling in process) or – and this very important to remember – they 'recover' without recourse to any treatment. The situation is rather similar in relation to the criminal justice literature and evidenced by the modest nature of the impact that accredited interventions have been shown to have on subsequent recidivism rates.

My view is that treatment almost certainly makes an important contribution to desisting from sexual offending, but it is only one element of the management toolkit, and a less significant element of that toolkit than practitioners would like to acknowledge. There is a risk that we become overly preoccupied with seeking the holy grail of treatment, by which I mean that we continually amend programmes in the hope of achieving ever greater treatment effects. I think it more likely – as

I said in Chapter 5 – that for high risk offenders with PPPD, we should change direction, and adopt a multi-modal approach to management (the diabetes model rather than the tonsillitis model, p. 107) that includes peer support, as well as a creative range of psychologically-informed approaches. To this end, Chapter 6 examines the impact of community management approaches, including external controls as well as a psychologically informed approach to adjusting the relational environment in order to maximise the possibilities of engagement and positive outcomes. The success of psychologically informed planning approaches in step 9 is heavily dependent on the accurate or meaningful completion of steps 1–8. There are very considerable dangers to the plan in focusing too heavily on developmental and relational processes if the risk factors have not been sufficiently explored and weighted; conversely, a stringent adherence to the risk analysis without the understanding of PPPDs runs a high risk of alienation and impasse in the plan.

Step 10: Test

Even when steps 1–9 have been completed in good faith, it is important to pause and reflect. Chapter 6 raised some questions about the strength of our belief in intuitively attractive risk management approaches, given the absence of evidence supporting them in terms of reducing sexual recidivism. Indeed, there is an emerging debate in the literature – as yet underpinned by little more than clinical or anecdotal evidence – that stringent risk management (rules regarding friendships and relationships, disclosure, notification, polygraphy) may be antithetical to relevant theoretical ideas about desistance and models of change for PPPD. To be balanced and fair, it is important to point out also that strengths based approaches such as the Good Lives Model also lack an empirical evidence base in relation to sexual recidivism.

The plan therefore needs to be tested: first as to whether it is in line with our theoretical ideas of change and desistance. For example, have we created too many obstacles to achieving social capital. Have we weighed up the likely risks versus the likely benefits of any particular action; are our rules avoidance and punishment oriented, or are they in line with approach goals and social reinforcement?

Second, rules carry the weight of authority but, as with parental authority, my advice is never to make a rule (a 'threat' in the eyes of the offender) that you are not prepared to carry out to its logical conclusion. Test your rule as to what is your threshold for action and what is your desired outcome. A commonly encountered example in the UK might be expectations around the offender disclosing an 'emerging intimate relationship' to you. Actually, practitioners are surprisingly poor at articulating exactly how this rule is defined, what they intend from this rule, and what they will do with the information once they receive it. For the sexual offender with PPPD, this provokes intense anxieties regarding their lack of control over the situation, confirming (in their eyes) authority figures as deceptively duplicitous and with the potential for humiliating experiences in relation to future disclosure. I am not trying to suggest that emerging relationships are irrelevant to risk; however, what may appear to the practitioner to be a fairly common sense approach to managing risk, may 'press the buttons' of the sexual offender leading to dysfunctional coping mechanisms. So for some of those offenders with a pervasive lack of trust in all authority figures, secrecy may seem like the only viable survival option, whilst for others, the anticipation of being 'failed' may provoke a desire to control the process of failure, to behave in such a way as to force the practitioner to return them to prison despite that not being the original purpose of the rule.

In summary, test whether the rules within the plan endorse reciprocity and social capital and throw out the rules that are not directly related to risk and therefore not crucial to the plan. Define the remaining rules in a way that anticipates the state of mind of the sexual offender as well as the state of mind of the practitioner.

Concluding thoughts about next steps

The book commenced with a brief overview of the social climate in which practitioners are working, and it seems appropriate to conclude with some reflections on the ways in which the public might be influencing this work with complex sexual offenders. The public is rightly focused on the trauma of the victims and the need to see justice at work in terms of retribution. Public protection – trying to ensure that we work in such a way as to prevent the commission of further sexual crimes by known sexual offenders – must remain at the forefront of our thinking. Therefore, although much of this book, and particularly the case vignettes within it, reflects a rather compassionate and empathic exploration of the psychological dilemmas faced by sexual offenders, this stance is meaningless unless it can be shown to be effective in keeping sexual recidivism to the lowest possible level.

There is no doubt that sexual offenders – just like other individuals who struggle with compulsive or shameful behaviours – can lie and deceive in response to kindness and professionalism. My own view therefore is that historical approaches that were exclusively oriented towards internal change by means of treatment have shown very little evidence of reliable change; in contrast, externally driven risk management controls undoubtedly have their place, and although it is difficult to disentangle the impact of such complex factors in society, they may well have contributed to the continuing reduction in sexual recidivism that is noted in North America and Europe.

However, there are two emerging difficulties, the first of which has been the focus of this book. That is, high risk sexual offenders with additional complexities in relation to their psychological functioning may respond poorly to mainstream approaches and, as a result, be denied opportunities to progress and to achieve a life worth living in the community. The hypothesis is that by adapting our approach and our models of management, many – albeit not all – such individuals can return to the community without putting the public at risk. However, the evidence is encouraging, but not yet definitive.

The second difficulty is one that is more entrenched and may well have a paradoxical impact on public protection; that is, the hypothesis that the vociferous opposition of the public to engage in a thinking manner about the question of sexual offenders in their midst may inadvertently increase rather than decrease risk. How might this happen?

- The public has long insisted that the monstrous nature of sexual offenders renders them 'other' and therefore not 'one of us;' this is one of the reasons why it has been so difficult to help adults protect their loved ones as they fail to be alert to the accurate risks.
- The drive to exclude sexual offenders from neighbourhoods seems like a victory but it is a short-sighted one; a displaced sexual offender, alone in a small flat and living incognito is potentially more risky to the neighbours than the clearly identified and tolerated sexual offender in supported group accommodation. For example, in the original Circle supporting a sexual offender in a rural village community, his identity and whereabouts was known to many people, his risk could therefore be managed and, ultimately, he was allowed to belong to that community.
- The combination of cognitive transformation ('that was me then, believe in who I am now') and social capital ('I am part of a community and a series of relationships which are reciprocal and to which I can make a meaningful contribution') are the key ingredients of desisting from repeat sexual offending; currently the public is hostile to such approaches. Practitioners, despite their genuine efforts to generate a meaningful risk management plan, are often pushed

into defensive rather than defensible rules and conditions; the line between the two is often very thin, but the outcomes may well be different. For example, third party disclosure, I would argue, is sometimes used as a defensive strategy and results in the recipient of the disclosure ejecting the offender, as we might catch and throw a 'hot potato,' with no discernible constructive outcome other than the false assurance of practitioners that we have been rigorous in our approach.

- Moral outrage does have an important place in society but it needs to remain outside the risk assessment process. Our anger on behalf of victims towards sexual offenders is meaningful and legitimate but, unfortunately, it has coloured our outlook for decades and impaired our ability to improve both our risk assessments and our treatment approaches, thereby diluting the impact we have had on sexual recidivism until very recently. For example, note the way in which practitioners have ignored the evidence that denial is not actually related to risk; denial is a moral imperative, not a risk imperative.

Sexual offenders belong to communities: they were born in districts, reared in local families, some of which were dysfunctional or traumatic; they were adversely influenced or ignored by neighbours, they truanted from our schools and were abused within our institutions, and at least a quarter of them were children and young adults under the age of 21 when they acquired their first sexual conviction. There are as many sexual offenders as there are individuals with schizophrenia, so although many spend years in prison, the majority are living down our streets. We cannot wish them all away, nor can we demonise them without further thought, when they are also people's sons, and occasionally their partners, or fathers of people who live around us. They are most certainly not to be viewed as victims and our society rightly inflicts punishment and retribution for their often-heinous crimes. Furthermore, we as practitioners are accountable to the public for our decisions and our professionalism; we owe the public the very highest standards of practice, and must be able to explain and justify our actions.

However, in my view, the very best practice and the very best outcomes will only be achieved when the community feels able to take some part ownership of and engagement with the challenge of managing sexual offenders in our midst and managing them safely. In a mature thinking partnership between the public, practitioners and sexual offenders, it should be possible to balance the absolutely requirement of public safety with a robust but compassionate engagement with the psychologically damaged but desisting sexual offender.

References

Davies, R. (1996). The inter-disciplinary network and the internal world of the offender. In (eds) C. Cordess and M. Cox, *Forensic Psychotherapy: Crime, Psychodynamics and the Offender Patient* (pp. 133–44). London: Jessica Kingsley.

Knauer, V., Walker, J. and Roberts, A. (2017). Offender personality disorder pathway: The impact of case consultation and formulation with probation staff. *The Journal of Forensic Psychiatry & Psychology*, *28*, 825–40.

Ministry of Justice (2015). *Working with Personality Disordered Offenders: A Practitioners Guide*. UK: National Offender Management Service. (www.gov.uk).

Shaw, J., Higgins, C. and Quartey, C. (2017). The impact of collaborative case formulation with high risk offenders with personality disorder. *The Journal of Forensic Psychiatry & Psychology*, *28*, 777–89.

Thornton, D. and d'Orazio, D. (2016). Advancing the evolution of sexual offender risk assessment. In (ed.) D. Boer, *The Wiley Handbook on the Theories, Assessment and Treatment of Sexual Offending. Volume I* (pp. 667–93). Chichester: John Wiley & Sons Ltd.

Index

Page entries in **bold** refer to tables.